1 America First or America Taxed? The Truth Behind Trump's Tariffs

Introduction
The Tariff Dilemma

In recent years, the word "tariff" has become a hot-button issue in American economic and political discourse. While tariffs have long been a tool of economic policy, they gained renewed attention under the administration of Donald Trump, who implemented a series of aggressive tariff measures under the banner of "America First." His argument was simple: tariffs would protect American industries, reduce trade deficits, and bring back jobs that had been lost to globalization. However, the reality of tariffs is far more complex, leading to both intended and unintended consequences that affected businesses, consumers, and international relations.

At the heart of the tariff debate lies a fundamental question: Did Trump's tariffs truly serve America's best interests, or did they ultimately burden the very people they were meant to protect? On the surface, tariffs appear to be a straightforward economic tool. By imposing taxes on imported goods, governments can discourage reliance on foreign products and encourage domestic manufacturing. The logic is that, by making foreign goods more expensive, American companies would have a competitive edge, leading to more jobs and stronger industries.

However, tariffs also come with significant downsides. When the U.S. imposes tariffs on imports, foreign countries often retaliate, leading to an escalating trade war. This was particularly evident in the U.S.-China trade conflict, where China responded to Trump's tariffs with countermeasures of its own, targeting American exports such as soybeans, automobiles, and electronics. This led to massive disruptions in key industries, particularly in agriculture, where farmers suddenly found themselves struggling to sell their crops in international markets.

Another critical issue is who ultimately pays for tariffs. While the Trump administration often claimed that China and other foreign exporters would bear the cost, economists widely agree that tariffs function as a tax on consumers and businesses. When importers are forced to pay higher taxes on goods, they pass those costs onto businesses and consumers in the form of higher prices. This was evident in various sectors, including the automobile and technology industries, where the cost of goods increased significantly due to new tariffs.

Beyond economic consequences, tariffs also reshaped America's global standing. Allies and trade partners, including Canada, Mexico, and the European Union, reacted negatively to Trump's tariff policies, leading to strained diplomatic relations. The imposition of tariffs on steel and aluminum, for example, angered Canada—one of the United States' closest allies—resulting in retaliatory tariffs on American products such as dairy, whiskey, and steel.

At the same time, some American industries did see benefits. Certain steel and aluminum manufacturers, for example, experienced an initial surge in demand as domestic production became more favorable. However, these benefits were unevenly distributed, and many businesses that relied on imported raw materials suffered from increased costs.

As the debate over Trump's tariffs continues, it remains unclear whether they strengthened or weakened the U.S. economy in the long run. Were they an effective tool for economic self-reliance and national security, or did they backfire by increasing costs and damaging international trade relations? This book seeks to uncover the full truth behind Trump's tariff policies, exploring their impact on businesses, consumers, and America's position in the global economy.

Chapter 1
The Origins of Trump's Tariff Strategy

Donald Trump's approach to trade policy was unlike that of any modern U.S. president. Throughout his 2016 presidential campaign, he repeatedly emphasized the need to revitalize American industry by reducing reliance on foreign imports. He argued that unfair trade practices, particularly by China and Mexico, had hollowed out U.S. manufacturing, leading to job losses and economic decline in key industrial regions. His solution? A bold, protectionist tariff strategy designed to make American products more competitive by imposing taxes on foreign goods. For Trump, tariffs were not just an economic tool but a central component of his "America First" philosophy, aimed at restoring economic independence and ensuring that the U.S. was no longer being, in his words, "ripped off" by other nations.

Trump's tariff strategy was built on a mix of historical protectionist policies and his personal views on economic nationalism. He drew inspiration from past American leaders who had used tariffs to strengthen domestic industries, such as the Smoot-Hawley Tariff Act of 1930, which aimed to protect American farmers and manufacturers during the Great Depression. However, while historical tariffs were often used in an era of limited globalization, Trump's strategy came at a time when the world's economies were deeply interconnected. His aggressive stance sparked debates among economists and policymakers about whether the U.S. could realistically shield itself from global trade dependencies or whether such measures would backfire by increasing costs for American consumers and businesses.

Another major influence on Trump's tariff strategy was his longstanding skepticism toward international trade agreements, which he often viewed as detrimental to American interests. He frequently criticized deals such as NAFTA (North American Free Trade Agreement) and the Trans-Pacific Partnership (TPP), arguing that they encouraged companies to move operations overseas, costing Americans their jobs. His administration wasted little time in renegotiating these agreements, culminating in the United States-Mexico-Canada Agreement (USMCA) as a replacement for NAFTA. However, his tariffs on China, the European Union, and other trade partners signaled that his approach went beyond just renegotiation—he was willing to engage in full-scale trade wars to reshape global trade relations. The question remained: Would these tariffs truly protect American industry, or would they set off a chain reaction of economic retaliation?

Tariffs in American History: A Legacy of Protectionism

Tariffs have played a crucial role in shaping the economic and political landscape of the United States since its founding. Throughout American history, tariffs have been used as a tool to protect domestic industries, generate government revenue, and influence international trade policies. While often seen as a means of economic self-sufficiency, tariffs have also sparked debates, economic conflicts, and even wars. Understanding the historical context of tariffs in America helps explain the motivations behind modern tariff policies, including those implemented by the Trump administration.

The early United States heavily relied on tariffs to fund the federal government. Before the implementation of the income tax in 1913, tariffs were the primary source of federal revenue. One of the first major tariff policies was the Tariff of 1789, which was enacted under President George Washington's administration. It was designed to raise funds for the newly established government while protecting emerging American industries from foreign competition, particularly from Britain. As the nation industrialized in the 19th century, tariffs became a key element of economic policy. The Tariff of 1816, for example, was the first explicitly protective tariff, aimed at shielding American manufacturers from the influx of cheap British goods following the War of 1812.

During the 19th century, tariffs became a deeply divisive issue, particularly between the industrial North and the agrarian South. Northern manufacturers favored high tariffs to protect their industries from European competition, while Southern states, which relied on exporting cash crops like cotton, opposed them because they led to retaliatory tariffs from other nations. The Tariff of 1828, also known as the "Tariff of Abominations," caused significant controversy by imposing high duties on imported goods, leading to economic hardship in the South. This tariff contributed to rising sectional tensions that eventually culminated in the Civil War.

In the late 19th and early 20th centuries, protectionist tariffs continued to shape American economic policy. The McKinley Tariff of 1890 and the Smoot-Hawley Tariff Act of 1930 were among the most notable. The Smoot-Hawley Tariff, enacted during the Great Depression, aimed to protect American farmers and manufacturers by imposing high import duties. However, it triggered a global trade war, as other countries retaliated with their own tariffs, worsening the economic downturn. This historical episode serves as a cautionary tale about the unintended consequences of aggressive protectionist policies.

Despite the lessons of the past, tariffs remained a key element of American trade policy throughout the 20th century. After World War II, the United States shifted toward a more open trade policy, supporting global trade agreements such as the General Agreement on Tariffs and Trade (GATT) and its successor, the World Trade Organization (WTO). However, protectionist tendencies resurfaced in the late 20th and early 21st centuries, particularly in response to concerns over job losses due to globalization and outsourcing. The resurgence of tariffs under the Trump administration can be seen as a continuation of America's historical struggle between free trade and protectionism.

The legacy of tariffs in American history highlights the ongoing debate over their effectiveness. While they have provided economic protection for certain industries, they have also led to retaliatory measures, increased consumer prices, and strained international relations. The question remains whether modern tariff policies can strike the right balance between economic nationalism and global trade cooperation.

The 2016 Campaign Promises: Economic Nationalism

Donald Trump's 2016 presidential campaign was centered around the idea of "America First," a slogan that resonated with millions of Americans who felt left behind by globalization and free trade agreements. A key pillar of this vision was economic nationalism, a policy framework that prioritizes domestic industries, job creation, and reduced reliance on foreign markets. Throughout his campaign, Trump promised to revive American manufacturing, reduce trade deficits, and bring jobs back to the United States by implementing a bold and aggressive trade policy—one that relied heavily on tariffs and the renegotiation of trade deals. His rhetoric suggested that previous administrations had sold out American workers by allowing China, Mexico, and other countries to take advantage of the U.S. through unfair trade practices.

One of Trump's main arguments was that free trade agreements had hollowed out American industry, leading to job losses in key manufacturing states like Michigan, Pennsylvania, and Wisconsin. He frequently cited the North American Free Trade Agreement (NAFTA) as a disastrous deal that encouraged companies to move production to Mexico, where labor was cheaper, at the expense of American workers. Similarly, he criticized China's entry into the World Trade Organization (WTO), arguing that it had allowed the Chinese government to manipulate currency, engage in unfair subsidies, and flood the U.S. market with cheap goods. Trump's campaign speeches were filled with promises to impose tariffs on countries that engaged in unfair trade practices, bring manufacturing jobs back, and force trading partners to renegotiate deals that he believed were detrimental to American interests.

Beyond rhetoric, Trump's campaign presented a clear economic vision that appealed to working-class Americans, especially in industrial states that had suffered from factory closures and job losses. His economic nationalism was framed as a rejection of the globalist policies championed by both Republican and Democratic administrations in previous decades. Trump argued that Washington elites had prioritized multinational corporations over American workers, allowing outsourcing and offshoring to devastate local communities. By using tariffs as an economic weapon, Trump promised to level the playing field and ensure that American businesses had a fair chance against foreign competitors. His supporters saw tariffs as a necessary tool to pressure companies into reshoring jobs and investing in American labor and manufacturing rather than seeking cheaper alternatives abroad.

As the campaign gained momentum, Trump doubled down on his promises by laying out specific policies, including a 45% tariff on Chinese imports and a 35% tariff on goods produced by American companies that outsourced jobs to Mexico. While many economists warned that such measures could lead to trade wars and higher consumer prices, Trump's message was clear: America would no longer be taken advantage of. His economic nationalism struck a chord with millions of voters who had grown frustrated with stagnant wages, job insecurity, and economic policies that seemed to favor large corporations over ordinary workers. Ultimately, his campaign promises on tariffs and trade helped him secure key battleground states and win the presidency. The challenge, however, was translating these promises into effective policies that would truly deliver on his vision of an economically independent and self-sufficient America.

Trade Wars: Trump's "Weapon of Choice"

Throughout his presidency, Donald Trump viewed trade wars not as a risk but as a strategic tool—a weapon to reshape global trade relations and reassert America's dominance in the international economy. Unlike previous administrations that sought to resolve trade disputes through diplomacy and multilateral negotiations, Trump believed that economic confrontation was necessary to force trading partners to make concessions. His administration aggressively used tariffs, trade restrictions, and renegotiated agreements to pressure countries like China, Mexico, Canada, and the European Union into what he perceived as fairer trade arrangements.

Trump's most significant trade war was with China, a country he repeatedly accused of currency manipulation, intellectual property theft, and unfair trade practices. In 2018, his administration imposed steep tariffs on $250 billion worth of Chinese imports, covering goods ranging from steel and aluminum to electronics and consumer products. China retaliated swiftly, slapping tariffs on U.S. agricultural products, automobiles, and industrial goods. This tit-for-tat escalation led to market uncertainty, economic instability, and increased costs for American businesses and consumers. Farmers, in particular, suffered significant losses as China's retaliatory tariffs cut off their access to one of the largest global markets for soybeans and other crops.

Despite the economic disruptions, Trump remained confident that his trade war with China was necessary, often claiming that "trade wars are good, and easy to win." He insisted that tariffs would force companies to bring production back to the United States, boost domestic manufacturing, and create jobs. However, economic data and industry reports suggested that instead of prompting businesses to reshore, many firms passed the cost of tariffs onto consumers or sought alternative supply chains in countries like Vietnam, India, and Mexico rather than returning operations to the U.S. While some American steel and aluminum manufacturers benefitted from the tariffs, industries that relied on imported raw materials—such as the auto sector—saw higher production costs and declining profits.

Beyond China, Trump also launched trade disputes with America's traditional allies, including Canada, Mexico, and the European Union. His administration imposed tariffs on steel and aluminum imports from these nations, arguing that protecting American metal industries was a matter of national security. This move angered long-standing trade partners and led to retaliatory tariffs on American exports, including dairy, whiskey, and machinery. The result was strained diplomatic relations and economic losses for U.S. businesses that depended on exports to these markets. The trade war also disrupted supply chains, forcing companies to rethink their sourcing and manufacturing strategies.

By the end of Trump's presidency, the results of his trade wars were mixed at best. While he succeeded in forcing China to agree to a Phase One trade deal in 2020, which included commitments to purchase more American goods, many of the tariffs remained in place, and economic tensions between the two nations persisted. The renegotiation of NAFTA into the United States-Mexico-Canada Agreement (USMCA) provided some wins for American workers, but the broader impact of Trump's tariff policies led to higher prices for consumers and economic uncertainty for businesses.

Ultimately, Trump's use of trade wars as a "weapon of choice" reflected his belief that economic aggression could yield better trade deals for America. However, the long-term consequences—rising costs, global retaliation, and an increasingly fragmented international trade system—left many questioning whether the approach truly served America's best interests.

The China Factor: Target or Scapegoat?

China played a central role in Donald Trump's trade policies, with his administration repeatedly framing it as the main threat to American economic security. From the moment he announced his presidential candidacy, Trump blamed China for America's declining manufacturing sector, rising trade deficits, and the loss of millions of jobs. His rhetoric resonated with many Americans, especially those in industrial states who had seen their communities devastated by outsourcing and factory closures. By targeting China with tariffs and sanctions, Trump positioned himself as a defender of American industry. However, a critical question remained throughout his presidency: Was China truly the root cause of America's economic struggles, or was it being used as a convenient scapegoat for broader issues in globalization and domestic economic policy?

One of the key arguments made by Trump and his advisors was that China had engaged in unfair trade practices for decades, harming American businesses and workers. They accused China of currency manipulation, meaning that Beijing deliberately devalued its currency to make its exports cheaper and more competitive in global markets. Additionally, the administration argued that China had violated intellectual property rights by forcing American companies to share technology in exchange for market access, engaging in cyber-espionage to steal trade secrets, and subsidizing state-owned enterprises to give them an unfair advantage. These concerns were not unique to Trump's administration—many previous U.S. leaders had voiced similar criticisms—but Trump was the first to use tariffs as an aggressive weapon to force China to change its policies.

In 2018, Trump launched a full-scale trade war against China, imposing tariffs on hundreds of billions of dollars' worth of Chinese goods. The goal was to pressure Beijing into making economic reforms and reducing the U.S. trade deficit with China. However, the Chinese government retaliated with its own tariffs, targeting key American industries such as agriculture, automobiles, and technology. Farmers, particularly soybean producers in the Midwest, suffered huge losses as China shifted its purchases to other countries like Brazil. In response, Trump's administration provided billions of dollars in subsidies to farmers to offset the impact, but the damage to supply chains and long-term trade relationships had already been done.

While China certainly engaged in some questionable trade practices, many economists and analysts argued that Trump's tariffs did little to address the core issues. Instead of bringing jobs back to America, many companies shifted production to other low-cost countries like Vietnam, India, and Mexico to avoid tariffs. The trade deficit with China did not significantly shrink, and instead, the cost of goods rose for American consumers and businesses. Moreover, the trade war disrupted global markets, creating uncertainty for investors and slowing economic growth in both the U.S. and China. Critics also pointed out that Trump's focus on China overlooked deeper structural issues, such as automation and the lack of investment in American workforce development, which had played a larger role in job losses than outsourcing alone.

By the end of Trump's presidency, the China factor remained unresolved. While the Phase One trade deal in 2020 resulted in some Chinese commitments to purchase more American goods, many tariffs remained in place, and tensions between the two countries persisted. Whether China was truly the root cause of America's economic challenges or just a scapegoat for deeper systemic problems remains a debated question, one that will likely shape U.S. trade policy for years to come.

Chapter 2
Winners and Losers of the Trade War

Donald Trump's trade war, particularly against China, created a complex economic landscape with both winners and losers. While the administration framed tariffs as a way to protect American industries and reduce dependence on foreign imports, the reality was far more nuanced. Certain sectors saw short-term gains, while others suffered significant disruptions, leading to job losses, increased costs, and strained global trade relations. The trade war's impact was felt across multiple industries, affecting everyone from farmers and factory workers to multinational corporations and consumers.

Among the winners were American steel and aluminum producers, who benefited from Trump's tariffs on imported metals. By raising the cost of foreign steel and aluminum, domestic manufacturers gained a competitive advantage, leading to higher production levels and increased profits in the short term. Some companies in the technology and defense sectors also benefited as the administration pushed for greater reliance on American-made components, particularly in critical areas such as semiconductors and 5G infrastructure. Additionally, certain companies that relocated their supply chains away from China found new opportunities in countries like Vietnam, India, and Mexico, reducing their dependency on Beijing.

However, the losers of the trade war far outnumbered the winners. American farmers, retailers, and manufacturers relying on imported raw materials were hit hardest. China's retaliatory tariffs severely impacted agriculture, especially soybean, pork, and dairy farmers, as China was previously the largest buyer of American agricultural exports. Many small businesses that depended on affordable imports faced rising costs, forcing them to either increase prices or absorb financial losses. Additionally, American consumers bore the brunt of higher prices, as tariffs led to inflated costs on everyday goods, from electronics to household appliances. While the trade war was intended to protect American jobs, many companies were forced to cut workforce expenses, delay expansion plans, or move operations overseas to mitigate the rising costs. In the end, the trade war produced a divided economic outcome, where select industries benefited while many others struggled under higher costs and economic uncertainty.

American Manufacturers: Shielded or Strangled?

When Donald Trump launched his aggressive tariff policies, one of his primary justifications was to protect American manufacturers from foreign competition. His administration argued that decades of outsourcing and globalization had weakened domestic production, allowing countries like China and Mexico to flood the U.S. market with cheaper goods. By imposing high tariffs on imported raw materials and finished products, Trump sought to give American manufacturers a competitive edge, encouraging companies to reshore production, create jobs, and strengthen the domestic supply chain. However, while some manufacturers benefited in the short term, the overall impact of the trade war proved to be a double-edged sword, shielding some industries while strangling others.

One of the biggest beneficiaries of Trump's tariff policies was the U.S. steel and aluminum industry. Before the tariffs, cheap steel imports—particularly from China—had driven many American mills out of business. The 25% tariff on steel and 10% tariff on aluminum helped boost domestic steel production, leading to an initial increase in demand, higher prices, and job growth within the industry. Similarly, certain manufacturers that relied on domestic raw materials, such as defense contractors and infrastructure companies, saw benefits from the tariffs as they faced less competition from foreign suppliers. In the short run, the tariffs also provided an incentive for some companies to relocate their supply chains back to the U.S., which aligned with Trump's broader goal of economic nationalism.

However, many other manufacturers suffered severe consequences due to the rising costs of raw materials. The tariffs on steel and aluminum, while beneficial to producers, significantly hurt industries that relied on these materials, such as the automotive, aerospace, and construction sectors. Companies that manufacture cars, machinery, and industrial equipment were suddenly paying much higher prices for essential materials, forcing them to either absorb the costs, raise prices, or cut jobs. Major manufacturers, including Ford and General Motors, reported billions of dollars in increased production costs due to tariffs, leading to slower growth, factory layoffs, and even plant closures. Many companies, instead of reshoring production, simply moved operations to countries like Vietnam and Mexico, where they could avoid the tariffs while still benefiting from lower labor costs.

Small and mid-sized manufacturers were particularly hard-hit by the trade war. Unlike larger corporations, which could absorb short-term financial losses, smaller businesses lacked the resources to cope with rising costs. Many of them relied on imported components to assemble final products, and the tariffs made these imports significantly more expensive. Some businesses faced supply chain disruptions, as retaliatory tariffs from China and the European Union reduced their ability to export American-made goods to key foreign markets. In many cases, the increased costs led to slower business expansion, workforce reductions, and even bankruptcies for smaller firms unable to adjust to the new economic reality.

Ultimately, the question of whether Trump's tariffs shielded or strangled American manufacturers depends on which industry is being examined. While steel and aluminum producers experienced a temporary revival, industries that relied on imported raw materials and global supply chains struggled under rising costs. In the broader picture, the tariffs did not spark a large-scale manufacturing renaissance as initially promised. Instead, they created market uncertainty, increased production expenses, and forced many businesses to make difficult decisions about their future operations. The long-term impact of these policies remains a subject of debate, but for many manufacturers, the tariffs felt more like a burden than a protective shield.

Farmers and the Agriculture Fallout

When Donald Trump initiated his trade war, one of the most severely affected groups in America was farmers. Agriculture has long been a cornerstone of the U.S. economy, with China, Canada, and Mexico among the largest buyers of American farm products. However, as Trump imposed steep tariffs on steel, aluminum, and Chinese imports, these trading partners retaliated with their own tariffs, directly targeting American agriculture. Farmers suddenly found themselves caught in the crossfire of a trade battle they had little control over, leading to significant financial losses, falling crop prices, and long-term uncertainty about the future of American farming.

One of the hardest-hit sectors was soybean farming. Before the trade war, China was the largest importer of American soybeans, purchasing over $12 billion worth of U.S. soybeans annually. However, in response to Trump's tariffs, China slapped a 25% retaliatory tariff on U.S. soybeans, effectively cutting American farmers out of their biggest market. With China turning to countries like Brazil and Argentina for its soybean supply, American soybean prices plummeted to their lowest levels in over a decade. Farmers who had previously relied on steady exports to China now faced mounting surpluses and financial instability, as they struggled to find alternative buyers for their crops.

Other agricultural sectors also suffered severe consequences. The dairy industry was hit by retaliatory tariffs from Mexico and Canada, two of its biggest export markets. Many dairy farmers had already been struggling with overproduction and falling milk prices, and the trade war only made matters worse, forcing some family-owned dairy farms to shut down. Pork producers faced similar challenges, as China and Mexico imposed tariffs on American pork, leading to a drop in demand and excess supply. Even the fruit and nut industry, which heavily relies on exports to China, experienced setbacks as shipments of almonds, pistachios, and cherries were delayed, canceled, or became too expensive for foreign buyers.

In response to the crisis, the Trump administration attempted to offset farmers' losses by rolling out billions of dollars in government subsidies through the Market Facilitation Program (MFP). The program provided direct payments to farmers affected by retaliatory tariffs, with over $28 billion allocated between 2018 and 2020. While this financial relief helped some farmers stay afloat, many argued that it was not a long-term solution. The payments did not fully compensate for lost trade relationships, and some small-scale farmers struggled to navigate the complex application process for receiving aid. Moreover, many farmers preferred stable trade relationships over temporary subsidies, as they feared that China's shift to alternative suppliers could permanently alter global agricultural trade patterns.

By the end of Trump's presidency, many farmers remained skeptical about the effectiveness of the trade war. While the Phase One trade deal signed in early 2020 committed China to purchasing more American farm products, it did not fully restore pre-trade war levels of agricultural exports. The damage had already been done— American farmers had lost market share, financial stability, and confidence in future trade agreements. For many in the agriculture sector, the trade war felt less like a strategic victory and more like an unnecessary economic burden, leaving them wondering whether the supposed gains of protectionist policies were worth the cost of lost global trust and economic hardship.

Consumers at the Checkout: Rising Costs

One of the most immediate and widespread effects of Donald Trump's trade war was the rising cost of everyday goods for American consumers. While the administration framed tariffs as a way to punish foreign countries for unfair trade practices and protect American jobs, the economic reality was that tariffs functioned as an import tax, which businesses often passed directly onto consumers. As tariffs were imposed on Chinese goods, steel, aluminum, and various raw materials, the cost of manufacturing and importing goods increased, resulting in higher prices at the checkout counter for millions of Americans.

The impact of tariffs was most noticeable in consumer electronics, household appliances, and automobiles, as these industries heavily rely on imported components. Products like smartphones, laptops, televisions, and washing machines saw price increases as manufacturers faced higher costs for imported circuit boards, batteries, and display screens. Major companies, including Apple and Whirlpool, publicly warned that tariffs would lead to increased prices for their products, making it more expensive for consumers to upgrade their devices or replace essential home appliances. Even American-made cars became pricier, as automakers like Ford and General Motors depended on imported steel and aluminum for production. The auto industry estimated that the tariffs added hundreds of dollars to the price of a new car, placing a greater financial burden on consumers already dealing with rising loan and interest rates.

Beyond electronics and automobiles, basic household goods and groceries also became more expensive. Many of the products found on supermarket shelves—such as canned goods, beverages, clothing, and furniture—contain imported materials or are manufactured overseas. As tariffs increased the cost of aluminum and steel, the price of soda, beer, and canned foods went up, since manufacturers had to pay more for packaging. Additionally, tariffs on textiles, plastics, and chemicals led to higher prices for clothing, shoes, and personal care products. A study by the Federal Reserve Bank of New York estimated that the trade war cost the average American household an additional $1,200 per year due to higher prices and reduced purchasing power.

For lower-income families, these rising costs were especially difficult to absorb. Unlike wealthy consumers who could afford to delay purchases or switch to premium alternatives, low- and middle-income households were disproportionately affected by price increases on essential goods. Even small increases in the cost of food, fuel, and household necessities put additional strain on family budgets, particularly in areas with already high living expenses. Retailers like Walmart and Target, which cater to budget-conscious shoppers, openly warned that tariffs would raise the cost of goods and reduce consumer spending power, potentially slowing down overall economic growth.

By the end of the trade war, the tariffs had failed to deliver on Trump's promise that foreign countries would bear the cost. Instead, American consumers paid the price, as businesses passed the increased costs onto them. While some industries may have benefited from protectionist policies, the vast majority of consumers faced rising costs, fewer choices, and reduced spending power. In the end, the trade war had a direct impact on millions of Americans' wallets, turning routine shopping trips into a more expensive and financially stressful experience.

Corporate America: Adaptation or Relocation?

Donald Trump's trade war forced Corporate America to make difficult choices in response to rising costs, supply chain disruptions, and economic uncertainty. While the administration aimed to push American companies toward domestic manufacturing, many businesses faced an impossible dilemma—should they adapt by absorbing higher costs and passing them onto consumers, or should they relocate production to avoid tariffs? For most companies, reshoring production back to the U.S. was not a viable option, as domestic labor and manufacturing costs remained significantly higher than in overseas markets. Instead, many corporations chose to adapt through price adjustments, cost-cutting measures, and supply chain restructuring, while others opted to relocate operations to different countries to bypass tariffs altogether.

For industries that relied heavily on Chinese imports and raw materials, the trade war meant higher operational costs. Corporations that could not easily relocate had to absorb these costs or shift them onto consumers. Companies like Apple, Whirlpool, and Ford publicly acknowledged that Trump's tariffs on Chinese-made components, steel, and aluminum would lead to higher prices for consumers. Some businesses attempted to reduce their dependence on Chinese suppliers by diversifying their sources, but this transition was costly and time-consuming. Additionally, multinational companies with complex global supply chains struggled to find alternative solutions that wouldn't result in logistical headaches. Beyond price hikes, many corporations resorted to cost-cutting measures, including workforce reductions, delaying expansion plans, and investing in automation to reduce reliance on expensive imported goods. The automotive and electronics industries, in particular, saw slowdowns in production and job losses, as manufacturers struggled with increased costs for raw materials. U.S. manufacturers that relied on global supply chains found themselves squeezed, caught between paying higher tariffs and remaining competitive in a fast-changing market.

Despite Trump's calls for reshoring jobs and manufacturing, most American companies chose to relocate production to other countries rather than return to the U.S. Countries like Vietnam, India, Thailand, and Mexico saw a surge in American investment, as companies sought to avoid tariffs on Chinese goods by shifting production to alternative locations. For example, tech companies such as Apple, HP, and Dell began moving manufacturing operations to Southeast Asia, reducing their reliance on Chinese factories. Vietnam, in particular, became a major beneficiary of the trade war, with exports to the U.S. growing significantly as manufacturers relocated operations there. Similarly, apparel and footwear brands, including Nike and Adidas, accelerated their moves away from Chinese production, setting up manufacturing hubs in countries with lower labor costs and fewer trade restrictions. The automotive industry also explored shifting parts production to Mexico, which, under the newly negotiated United States-Mexico-Canada Agreement (USMCA), provided a more stable environment for manufacturing without the high tariffs imposed on Chinese imports. In the end, Trump's trade war did not lead to a mass return of manufacturing to the U.S., as many of his supporters had hoped. Instead, businesses adjusted by raising prices, cutting costs, or relocating to countries with more favorable trade conditions. While some American industries—such as steel and aluminum—saw short-term gains, the broader economy faced increased prices, supply chain disruptions, and job losses in sectors heavily reliant on global trade. The trade war, rather than revitalizing American manufacturing, accelerated a shift away from China but failed to bring industries back home, leaving Corporate America in a state of adaptation rather than resurgence.

Chapter 3
The Global Trade Chessboard

Donald Trump's trade war was not just a battle between the United States and China—it had global implications, reshaping trade alliances, shifting supply chains, and forcing countries to rethink their economic strategies. As the U.S. imposed tariffs on Chinese goods, China responded in kind, targeting American exports. But the effects of this conflict were felt far beyond these two economic giants. Traditional allies such as Canada, Mexico, and the European Union were also drawn into the dispute, as Trump's tariffs on steel and aluminum sparked retaliatory measures. Other nations saw opportunities to capitalize on the disruption, with countries like Vietnam and India positioning themselves as alternative manufacturing hubs for companies looking to escape U.S.-China tensions. The global trade system, built on decades of cooperation and free trade agreements, was suddenly thrown into a period of uncertainty.

In response to the trade war, major economies adapted by forming new trade agreements and strengthening existing alliances. While Trump withdrew the U.S. from the Trans-Pacific Partnership (TPP), the remaining countries moved forward without American involvement, rebranding the deal as the Comprehensive and Progressive Agreement for Trans-Pacific Partnership (CPTPP). This allowed Asia-Pacific nations to expand trade among themselves, reducing their reliance on the U.S. market. Meanwhile, China deepened its economic ties with Europe and Latin America, negotiating new trade agreements to counterbalance the impact of American tariffs. The European Union also sought to protect its interests by signing major trade deals with Japan and Canada, ensuring that it remained a key player in global commerce. These shifting alliances indicated that while the U.S. was attempting to assert its dominance, other nations were finding ways to work around American trade policies, reducing their dependence on the world's largest economy.

Despite Trump's belief that trade wars were "good and easy to win," the reality proved more complicated. The tariffs caused disruptions in global supply chains, increased manufacturing costs, and created economic instability in both developed and emerging markets. Some American businesses that relied on global trade found themselves at a disadvantage as foreign competitors gained an edge through newly established trade partnerships. Additionally, smaller economies that depended on exports to both the U.S. and China faced difficulties as they navigated the uncertain economic landscape. In the end, the trade war did not lead to a decisive victory for the U.S.; rather, it contributed to a fragmented global trade system where countries sought to diversify their economic relationships. The chessboard had shifted, but the outcome remained unclear, leaving the world in a delicate balance between cooperation and economic nationalism.

Retaliation from China and the EU

When Donald Trump launched his aggressive tariff policies, he assumed that other nations would concede to U.S. demands or negotiate trade deals on his terms. However, instead of backing down, China and the European Union (EU) responded with strong retaliatory measures, escalating the trade war and further complicating global economic relations. These countermeasures were not only aimed at hurting the U.S. economy but also at signaling to the world that America's trading partners would not be bullied into submission. The retaliation from China and the EU had significant consequences for American businesses, farmers, and consumers, ultimately making the trade war more costly than originally anticipated.

China, as the primary target of Trump's tariffs, responded swiftly and strategically. The Chinese government imposed tariffs on over $110 billion worth of American goods, focusing on industries that were vital to Trump's political base, particularly agriculture and manufacturing. One of the biggest blows came in the form of a 25% tariff on American soybeans, which had been one of the U.S.'s largest exports to China. Prior to the trade war, China accounted for nearly 60% of U.S. soybean exports, but after the tariffs, Beijing turned to Brazil and Argentina for its soybean supply, leaving American farmers with unsold surpluses and collapsing prices. Many Midwestern farmers, already struggling with rising production costs and uncertain markets, faced bankruptcy despite billions of dollars in government subsidies meant to offset their losses. Beyond agriculture, China's tariffs targeted automobiles, aircraft, and industrial equipment, hurting companies like Boeing, Caterpillar, and General Motors. As American firms saw declining exports to China, some companies even considered relocating production to avoid tariffs, with Harley-Davidson shifting some of its operations overseas. China also implemented non-tariff barriers, such as increased bureaucratic regulations, stricter customs inspections, and delays in approving licenses for American businesses operating in China. These measures created an uncertain business environment, discouraging further U.S. investment in the Chinese market.

While Trump initially focused on China, his trade war also strained relations with key allies in the European Union. When the U.S. imposed tariffs on steel and aluminum imports, the EU retaliated with tariffs on $3.2 billion worth of American products, strategically targeting goods produced in politically significant U.S. states. Among the affected items were American whiskey, Harley-Davidson motorcycles, Levi's jeans, and agricultural products like peanuts and orange juice. The goal was to pressure American lawmakers and businesses to push back against Trump's trade policies, showing that the EU would not tolerate unilateral tariffs. In addition to tariffs, the EU strengthened trade alliances with other countries, such as signing the EU-Japan Economic Partnership Agreement, ensuring that European businesses had alternative markets in case the U.S. continued its protectionist policies. The EU also increased diplomatic cooperation with China, presenting a united front against Trump's trade aggression. Instead of isolating China economically, Trump's tariffs pushed the EU and China closer together, giving Beijing new trade opportunities while American exporters struggled with market restrictions. By the time Trump left office, his trade war had caused widespread economic disruptions without securing clear victories. Instead of forcing China and the EU to submit, the tariffs led to greater economic uncertainty, increased consumer prices, and weakened U.S. trade relations with allies. Many of the tariffs remained in place under the Biden administration, signaling that the long-term impact of Trump's trade policies would continue to shape global trade for years to come.

Shifting Trade Alliances and New Agreements

Donald Trump's trade war not only disrupted long-standing economic relationships but also forced countries around the world to rethink their trade strategies. As the United States imposed tariffs on key trading partners and withdrew from multilateral agreements, other nations responded by forging new alliances and strengthening existing trade partnerships. The instability caused by the tariffs prompted countries to seek alternative economic arrangements, reshaping the global trade landscape in ways that reduced reliance on the U.S. market. This shift had long-term implications for American businesses, as traditional allies and economic partners sought to minimize their exposure to the unpredictability of U.S. trade policies.

One of the most significant changes came in the Asia-Pacific region. When Trump withdrew the United States from the Trans-Pacific Partnership (TPP) in 2017, the remaining countries moved forward without American involvement, renaming the agreement as the Comprehensive and Progressive Agreement for Trans-Pacific Partnership (CPTPP). This deal included major economies such as Japan, Canada, Australia, and Vietnam, creating one of the largest free-trade zones in the world. Without U.S. participation, American businesses lost preferential access to these markets, while competitors from member countries gained trade advantages. China, seeing an opportunity to expand its influence, later joined the Regional Comprehensive Economic Partnership (RCEP), a separate trade agreement that brought together 15 nations, including Japan and South Korea. These agreements allowed Asian economies to deepen their trade ties while reducing their reliance on U.S. exports and investments.

Europe also adapted to the shifting trade environment by pursuing its own strategic partnerships. The European Union strengthened its trade relations with Canada through the Comprehensive Economic and Trade Agreement (CETA), while also finalizing a major agreement with Japan, known as the EU-Japan Economic Partnership Agreement. These agreements facilitated tariff reductions and streamlined trade flows, making it easier for European companies to do business with international partners while bypassing the economic uncertainty caused by Trump's tariffs. In response to the U.S. imposing tariffs on steel and aluminum, the EU also worked more closely with China, expanding trade ties to counterbalance the impact of American restrictions. This shift demonstrated that while Trump sought to use tariffs as leverage, many countries were unwilling to negotiate under economic pressure and instead sought alternative trade routes that reduced their dependence on the United States.

In North America, the renegotiation of the North American Free Trade Agreement (NAFTA) into the United States-Mexico-Canada Agreement (USMCA) reflected Trump's preference for bilateral or regional agreements over broader multilateral deals. While USMCA preserved much of NAFTA's original structure, it included provisions that increased labor protections and encouraged more domestic automobile production within the U.S. However, the uncertainty caused by Trump's threats to withdraw from NAFTA altogether had already led businesses to rethink their supply chains. Many companies, rather than waiting for trade disputes to settle, diversified their operations by increasing investments in regions less affected by U.S. tariffs. The broader effect of these shifting alliances and new agreements was that the U.S., once the dominant force in global trade, found itself sidelined in many economic negotiations. By the end of Trump's presidency, America's role in international trade had changed, with former allies and trade partners increasingly looking for ways to reduce their dependence on U.S. policies.

The Supply Chain Crisis: Unintended Consequences

Donald Trump's trade war and tariff policies had far-reaching consequences, many of which were unintended and disruptive to global supply chains. While the administration sought to encourage companies to bring production back to the United States, the reality was that businesses faced mounting costs, logistical challenges, and delays that created a ripple effect across industries. The trade war exacerbated existing vulnerabilities in supply chains, leading to higher prices, shortages, and inefficiencies that ultimately harmed American businesses and consumers alike. Instead of strengthening domestic manufacturing, the tariffs forced companies to make difficult choices, such as absorbing higher costs, relocating to alternative markets, or dealing with massive supply chain disruptions that affected their ability to operate efficiently.

One of the biggest consequences of the trade war was the increased cost of raw materials and essential components. Many American manufacturers relied on imports from China, Mexico, and other countries for critical parts, including semiconductors, machinery, and electronic components. When Trump's tariffs went into effect, businesses suddenly faced steep price increases on these imports, making production more expensive. As a result, companies in industries such as automotive, technology, and consumer goods had to decide whether to raise prices for consumers or cut costs elsewhere, often leading to job losses or decreased investment in innovation. The auto industry, in particular, suffered from the higher cost of steel and aluminum, which made manufacturing more expensive and led to price hikes on vehicles, ultimately reducing consumer demand.

The trade war also triggered a wave of supply chain disruptions as companies scrambled to restructure their sourcing strategies. While Trump's tariffs were meant to punish China, many American businesses did not simply bring production back to the U.S. due to higher domestic labor and manufacturing costs. Instead, they sought alternative production hubs in Vietnam, India, Thailand, and Mexico, shifting their supply chains to avoid tariffs on Chinese imports. However, these rapid transitions were not seamless. Many of these countries lacked the infrastructure and production capacity to handle the massive demand that had previously been absorbed by China. This led to delays, production inefficiencies, and bottlenecks that affected industries worldwide. Additionally, trade uncertainty made companies hesitant to invest in long-term solutions, leading to a climate of instability that hurt global trade.

The unintended consequences of the supply chain crisis became even more apparent during the COVID-19 pandemic, when businesses that had already been struggling with trade war disruptions found themselves unable to secure key supplies. The reliance on a fragile and shifting supply chain made it difficult for industries to adapt to sudden global shutdowns. Essential goods, such as medical equipment, electronics, and consumer products, faced severe shortages, while businesses struggled with shipping delays and logistical backlogs. The combination of trade war policies and pandemic-related disruptions exposed the weaknesses of global supply chains, forcing companies and governments to rethink their approach to trade and production. By the end of Trump's presidency, the U.S. had not achieved a manufacturing revival but had instead witnessed a fractured supply chain system that contributed to inflation, product shortages, and long-term economic uncertainty.

The Future of Globalization: Slowdown or Reset?

Donald Trump's trade war and protectionist policies triggered a global debate about the future of globalization, forcing governments, businesses, and consumers to reconsider their reliance on international trade networks. For decades, globalization had been seen as an inevitable force, driving economic growth, innovation, and interconnected supply chains. However, the disruptions caused by tariffs, trade restrictions, and geopolitical tensions raised an important question: was globalization slowing down, or was it undergoing a fundamental reset? While Trump's policies did not entirely dismantle global trade, they exposed the vulnerabilities of over-reliance on foreign markets and pushed many countries to reconsider their economic strategies.

One of the most immediate effects of Trump's trade war was the fragmentation of international supply chains. As tariffs increased the cost of importing goods from China and other trading partners, companies sought alternatives to reduce dependency on any single country. This shift led to regionalization of trade, with businesses moving production to Vietnam, India, Mexico, and other emerging economies. Some corporations also explored the idea of reshoring, or bringing manufacturing back to the United States, though this proved to be an expensive and complex process. Instead of a complete retreat from globalization, what emerged was a realignment of trade relationships, where companies diversified their suppliers and governments invested in greater economic self-sufficiency. This shift suggested that globalization was not disappearing, but it was evolving into a more decentralized and strategically controlled model.

At the same time, countries sought to strengthen regional trade agreements in response to U.S. tariffs and shifting alliances. The European Union pursued new trade deals with Japan, Canada, and Latin America, while China accelerated efforts to expand its influence through the Belt and Road Initiative and its participation in the Regional Comprehensive Economic Partnership (RCEP). These agreements allowed economies to bypass U.S. trade barriers and create alternative markets for exports and investments. As a result, while the U.S. attempted to enforce protectionist policies, much of the world continued to integrate economically, albeit in new and adjusted ways. Rather than seeing a complete slowdown of globalization, the world experienced a reset—one in which new trade routes and partnerships emerged while global power dynamics shifted.

By the time Trump left office, the debate over globalization had fundamentally changed. The COVID-19 pandemic further exposed the fragility of global supply chains, reinforcing the idea that nations must balance economic integration with national security and resilience. Policymakers across the world began focusing on reducing dependency on foreign suppliers, particularly in critical sectors such as technology, pharmaceuticals, and energy. While globalization is unlikely to disappear entirely, it is becoming more selective, more regionalized, and more politically driven. Trump's trade policies accelerated this transformation, demonstrating that while free trade remains vital for economic growth, countries are increasingly prioritizing self-sufficiency and strategic independence. The future of globalization will not be defined by a simple continuation or a complete reversal, but rather by a recalibration of economic priorities, where nations seek to balance the benefits of global trade with the risks of over-dependence on any single economy.

Chapter 4
The Economic Impact on Main Street and Wall Street

Donald Trump's trade war had a profound impact on both Main Street and Wall Street, creating a divide between the everyday American worker and small businesses on one side and large corporations and financial markets on the other. While Trump's tariffs were promoted as a means to revive domestic manufacturing, reduce trade deficits, and create jobs, their consequences played out differently across the economy. For many American households, the trade war resulted in higher prices, job uncertainty, and financial strain, while on Wall Street, investors experienced volatile stock markets, shifting corporate strategies, and fluctuating economic growth expectations. The trade policies created winners and losers, with some sectors benefiting while others struggled under the weight of rising costs and economic unpredictability.

For small businesses and local communities—the heart of Main Street America—the impact of tariffs was largely negative. Many small manufacturers relied on imported raw materials, such as steel, aluminum, and electronic components, and when tariffs increased the cost of these goods, it became harder to remain competitive. Retailers also faced challenges as higher import costs led to increased prices on consumer products, forcing many businesses to either absorb the additional costs or pass them on to customers. Farmers, particularly in the Midwest, suffered from China's retaliatory tariffs on U.S. agricultural exports, losing access to one of their largest markets. Despite government subsidies aimed at cushioning the blow, many farmers and small business owners faced financial hardship and uncertainty about their future in an increasingly unstable trade environment.

On the other hand, Wall Street reacted with mixed signals. While some industries, particularly domestic steel and aluminum producers, initially saw stock price increases, the broader market experienced significant volatility due to uncertainty surrounding global trade relations. Large multinational corporations, particularly those in the tech and automotive sectors, faced disruptions as they navigated shifting supply chains and increased production costs. Investors feared that prolonged trade disputes could slow economic growth, leading to market downturns and lower corporate earnings. At the same time, some companies saw opportunities to adjust their operations, expand into alternative markets, or capitalize on tariff exemptions, demonstrating the resilience of large corporations in adapting to new economic realities. By the end of Trump's presidency, the economic impact of the trade war remained a topic of debate, as Main Street struggled with rising costs and job losses, while Wall Street continued its pursuit of profits amidst an evolving global trade landscape.

Stock Market Reactions to Tariff Announcements

The stock market is highly sensitive to economic policies, and Trump's tariff announcements created a rollercoaster of volatility on Wall Street. While his administration promoted tariffs as a way to strengthen domestic industries and reduce trade imbalances, financial markets reacted with uncertainty, sharp fluctuations, and increased investor anxiety. Each new round of tariffs—whether on China, Europe, or North American trade partners—triggered market selloffs, rebounds, and shifts in investment strategies, as investors attempted to gauge the long-term economic impact. The unpredictability of trade policy became a defining characteristic of Trump's presidency, leading to one of the most turbulent periods for global financial markets.

One of the most immediate effects of tariff announcements was market-wide selloffs, particularly in sectors most vulnerable to trade restrictions. Technology, automotive, and manufacturing companies were hit hardest, as many relied on global supply chains and imported components to maintain production and profitability. When Trump announced tariffs on $200 billion worth of Chinese imports in 2018, the Dow Jones Industrial Average (DJIA) dropped nearly 800 points in a single day, as investors feared the repercussions for multinational corporations like Apple, General Motors, and Boeing. Similar market dips occurred whenever China retaliated with its own tariffs, especially when they targeted U.S. agriculture, aviation, and industrial machinery, further increasing economic uncertainty.

Despite initial downturns, certain sectors benefited from the trade war, creating a divergence in stock market performance. Domestic steel and aluminum producers saw stock price gains following tariffs on foreign metals, as investors believed these industries would enjoy a short-term competitive advantage. Companies in the defense sector also performed well, as Trump's focus on national security and reducing reliance on Chinese technology led to increased government contracts for domestic suppliers. However, these gains were often offset by broader market losses, as corporate earnings projections declined, consumer prices increased, and supply chain inefficiencies emerged, affecting investor confidence in long-term economic stability.

The Federal Reserve also played a role in stock market reactions to trade policies, as economic uncertainty prompted changes in monetary policy. In response to market instability caused by tariffs, the Fed adjusted interest rates multiple times between 2018 and 2019, attempting to stimulate economic growth and counterbalance trade-related slowdowns. While lower interest rates helped support stock prices in the short term, they also signaled potential economic weakness, adding to investor concerns about recession risks. Many analysts warned that prolonged trade disputes could lead to reduced corporate investment, slower GDP growth, and job losses, further dampening market optimism.

By the end of Trump's presidency, stock markets had recovered from trade war shocks, but the uncertainty surrounding tariffs had lasting effects on investment decisions and global trade relationships. Companies diversified supply chains, moved production away from China, and adopted new risk management strategies to mitigate future trade policy disruptions. While Wall Street remained resilient, the volatility caused by tariff announcements underscored the fragility of global financial markets when subjected to sudden and aggressive economic policies. The trade war's legacy on stock markets served as a reminder of how deeply interconnected global economies are, and how policy shifts can ripple across industries, investor confidence, and overall financial stability.

Small Businesses: Surviving the Cost Surge

Small businesses were among the hardest hit by Donald Trump's trade war, as they struggled to absorb the rising costs of imported goods, raw materials, and manufacturing components. Unlike large corporations, which had global supply chains, greater financial reserves, and the ability to shift production overseas, small businesses operated on tighter profit margins and had fewer resources to adjust to sudden economic shocks. For many, the increased tariffs on Chinese imports, steel, aluminum, and other essential products led to higher expenses, reduced competitiveness, and difficult financial decisions. The trade war was framed as a measure to protect American industries, but for many small businesses, it felt more like an economic burden rather than a benefit.

One of the primary challenges small businesses faced was the increased cost of goods and materials. Many relied on imported raw materials, parts, or finished products to run their operations, and when tariffs were imposed, these costs surged. For example, businesses in manufacturing, retail, and construction saw price hikes in steel, aluminum, and electronic components, making it more expensive to produce and sell goods. Since small businesses lacked the buying power of large corporations, they often had to pay even higher rates for materials, putting them at a competitive disadvantage. Some tried to pass the increased costs onto consumers, but this approach was risky, as it made their products less attractive compared to larger competitors who could absorb short-term losses.

Beyond rising material costs, small businesses also faced disruptions in their supply chains. As tariffs made imports from China more expensive, many businesses tried to source products from alternative markets, such as Vietnam, India, and Mexico. However, shifting suppliers was not easy, as new trade relationships took time to establish, and alternative suppliers could not always meet demand. This led to delays, production slowdowns, and inventory shortages, all of which affected revenue and customer satisfaction. Additionally, many small businesses lacked the logistical expertise to navigate new import regulations, customs procedures, and trade agreements, further complicating their ability to adapt.

To survive the cost surge, small business owners had to make tough financial choices. Many were forced to cut operating expenses, reduce staff, or delay expansion plans in order to stay afloat. Others sought loans or financial assistance, though rising interest rates and economic uncertainty made borrowing riskier. The U.S. government attempted to provide relief through subsidies and small business aid programs, but many entrepreneurs argued that these measures were not enough to offset long-term losses caused by trade disruptions. Some businesses that relied heavily on international trade were forced to close, as they could no longer compete in a market dominated by larger, more resilient corporations.

By the end of the trade war, many small businesses had either adapted, downsized, or shut down entirely. While some found ways to diversify their supply chains or increase domestic sourcing, others struggled to recover from the economic uncertainty caused by tariffs. The experience demonstrated that while protectionist trade policies may have been designed to support American industry, they often disproportionately harmed small businesses, which lacked the financial flexibility to endure prolonged economic instability.

Inflation and the Tariff Connection

Donald Trump's trade war and the resulting tariffs played a significant role in driving inflation in the U.S. economy. While the administration framed tariffs as a tool to protect American industries and jobs, the reality was that these import taxes led to higher costs for businesses and consumers alike. By imposing tariffs on Chinese goods, steel, aluminum, and various other imported materials, the prices of essential goods and raw materials increased across multiple industries, contributing to inflationary pressures. As businesses struggled to absorb these rising costs, they had little choice but to pass them on to consumers, leading to a noticeable rise in the cost of living for many Americans.

One of the most immediate effects of the tariffs was the higher cost of production for manufacturers. Many industries in the U.S. rely on imported components and raw materials to produce goods, and the added tariffs made these inputs significantly more expensive. The automobile, technology, and construction sectors were particularly affected, as they depend heavily on steel, aluminum, and electronic components from abroad. With tariffs raising the price of these materials, the cost of producing cars, appliances, electronics, and even housing skyrocketed, making everything from vehicles to home construction more expensive. This price surge rippled through the economy, contributing to overall inflationary pressures and reducing the purchasing power of consumers.

Beyond industrial goods, the tariffs also directly impacted consumer prices for everyday products. Many household essentials, electronics, clothing, and groceries contain imported components or are manufactured abroad before being sold in the U.S. With tariffs in place, retailers and suppliers faced increased costs, which they passed down to shoppers in the form of higher prices at the checkout counter. Even essential food items, such as canned goods and beverages, became more expensive due to tariffs on aluminum used in packaging. A study by the Federal Reserve Bank of New York estimated that the trade war cost the average American household an additional $1,200 per year, further straining household budgets and reducing discretionary spending.

The link between tariffs and inflation became even more evident when businesses adjusted wages and employment strategies in response to rising costs. Small businesses, in particular, struggled to keep prices stable while maintaining profitability, forcing them to cut jobs, delay expansions, or reduce wage increases. This had a direct impact on economic growth, as consumer spending weakened in response to rising prices and job uncertainty. The Federal Reserve also took monetary policy actions to counteract inflationary effects, leading to changes in interest rates that influenced everything from mortgages to credit card debt. The combination of higher prices, supply chain disruptions, and market volatility created an economic environment where inflation remained a persistent concern.

By the end of Trump's presidency, inflationary pressures caused by tariffs had not fully subsided, and many of the price increases remained in place. While the trade war was meant to revitalize American industry, its broader economic impact led to inflation that hurt businesses and consumers alike. The experience demonstrated how tariffs, when implemented on a large scale, do not just affect international trade but have lasting consequences on the cost of living, economic stability, and consumer confidence.

Job Growth vs. Job Losses: The Real Impact

Donald Trump's trade war and tariff policies were introduced with the promise of reviving American industries and creating jobs, but the actual impact on employment was more complex. While some industries, such as steel and aluminum, saw short-term job growth due to tariff protections, others—especially those relying on imported goods and raw materials—experienced job losses, factory shutdowns, and hiring freezes. The effects of tariffs on employment were uneven, with certain sectors benefiting while others struggled under the weight of rising costs, supply chain disruptions, and reduced global demand. Instead of leading to a large-scale return of jobs to the U.S., the trade war created uncertainty that slowed investment and hiring, making the overall impact on employment a mixed outcome.

One of the key beneficiaries of the tariffs was the domestic steel and aluminum industry, which had suffered for years due to competition from cheaper foreign imports. When the Trump administration imposed a 25% tariff on steel and a 10% tariff on aluminum, American steelmakers saw a temporary boost in production, leading to increased hiring. Companies like U.S. Steel announced plans to reopen mills and hire new workers, and for a brief period, employment in steel-producing regions saw an uptick. Similarly, some manufacturers that relied on American-made materials benefitted from reduced competition, allowing them to expand their workforce. However, the gains in these industries were offset by greater losses in sectors that relied on steel and aluminum for production, such as the automotive, aerospace, and construction industries, where higher input costs led to job cuts instead of job creation.

For industries that depended on global supply chains, tariffs created major challenges that resulted in layoffs, hiring freezes, and business closures. Automakers, machinery manufacturers, and electronics companies faced rising costs for essential components, making production more expensive. Companies like General Motors and Ford responded by cutting jobs and closing plants, citing higher costs as one of the factors in their decisions. Small and mid-sized manufacturers, which lacked the resources of larger corporations, struggled to stay profitable, leading to thousands of job losses across multiple states. Retail businesses were also affected, as tariffs on Chinese-made consumer goods led to higher prices, reducing consumer spending and forcing some stores to downsize or shut down entirely.

Agriculture was another sector that experienced significant job losses due to the trade war. When China imposed retaliatory tariffs on U.S. soybeans, pork, dairy, and other farm products, American farmers lost access to a major export market, leading to financial hardship and farm closures. With reduced demand and plummeting prices, many farmers had to lay off workers or abandon production altogether. The Trump administration attempted to offset these losses with billions in government subsidies, but many in the agriculture industry argued that stable trade relationships would have been far more beneficial than temporary financial aid.

By the end of Trump's presidency, job growth in certain protected industries had been outweighed by job losses in sectors affected by tariffs and trade disruptions. The uncertainty surrounding trade policy also discouraged companies from making long-term investments in hiring and expansion. Instead of delivering a major boost to American employment, the trade war resulted in a net economic slowdown, leaving many workers caught in the crossfire of shifting trade policies.

Chapter 5
Tariffs and National Security: A Justified Move?

The Trump administration framed tariffs not just as an economic tool but also as a matter of national security, arguing that reducing dependence on foreign goods would strengthen America's strategic industries. The justification for imposing tariffs on steel, aluminum, and technology components was that these industries were vital to the country's defense and long-term security. Trump and his advisors contended that cheap foreign imports had weakened domestic production capabilities, making the U.S. vulnerable in critical areas such as military equipment, infrastructure, and advanced technology. By using national security as a rationale for tariffs, the administration aimed to revitalize domestic industries and reduce reliance on geopolitical rivals like China.

However, the move was highly controversial, drawing criticism from economists, industry leaders, and international allies. Many experts argued that national security concerns were being used as a cover for economic protectionism, rather than addressing legitimate threats. The tariffs on steel and aluminum, for example, not only targeted China but also affected longstanding allies such as Canada, the European Union, and Japan, leading to diplomatic tensions. Critics pointed out that America's security alliances depended on strong economic relationships, and alienating allies over trade disputes could have unintended consequences. Furthermore, many industries that relied on imported materials faced higher costs, making them less competitive and potentially harming America's long-term economic strength.

Despite the backlash, the administration doubled down on its national security argument, particularly in sectors such as technology and telecommunications. The U.S. took aggressive steps to limit China's influence in 5G networks, semiconductor production, and artificial intelligence, citing concerns over cybersecurity, espionage, and intellectual property theft. Restrictions on Chinese companies like Huawei and increased scrutiny on foreign investment were seen as necessary moves to protect America's technological edge. However, these measures also had economic side effects, disrupting global supply chains and creating uncertainty for tech companies. The question remained: were tariffs a necessary tool for safeguarding national security, or did they do more harm than good by straining alliances and raising costs for American industries?

Steel and Aluminum Tariffs: Strengthening Defense?

The Trump administration justified the steel and aluminum tariffs as a national security measure, arguing that reliance on foreign imports weakened the United States' ability to produce essential materials for military and infrastructure needs. By imposing a 25% tariff on steel and a 10% tariff on aluminum in 2018 under Section 232 of the Trade Expansion Act of 1962, the administration claimed it was taking decisive action to revitalize domestic production, protect American workers, and ensure the country's defense capabilities were not at risk. Trump argued that foreign competition, particularly from China, had led to the closure of many U.S. steel plants, making the country vulnerable in the event of geopolitical conflict or economic disruption.

While the tariffs did provide a temporary boost to domestic steel and aluminum manufacturers, the broader economic consequences were more complicated. In the short term, American steelmakers saw an increase in demand, as domestic production became more competitive without cheaper foreign imports flooding the market. Companies such as U.S. Steel and Nucor Corporation announced investments in new plants and job creation, leading to optimism in the industrial sector. Supporters of the tariffs pointed to historical precedents where strong domestic steel industries were considered crucial during wartime production, reinforcing the argument that self-sufficiency in metals was a matter of national defense. The administration also claimed that these tariffs would reduce America's dependence on adversarial nations, particularly China, which was accused of dumping excess steel into global markets at artificially low prices.

However, the tariffs had unintended negative consequences, particularly for industries that relied on steel and aluminum as raw materials. The automotive, aerospace, and construction sectors faced rising costs, as they had to pay higher prices for domestic metals or absorb the added costs of tariffs on imported materials. Major U.S. automakers such as Ford and General Motors reported that the tariffs added billions of dollars to their expenses, forcing them to adjust production strategies, increase prices for consumers, and, in some cases, cut jobs to offset costs. Similarly, manufacturers of machinery, canned goods, and household appliances struggled with price hikes, making their products less competitive both domestically and internationally. The very industries that the tariffs were meant to protect were now facing higher operational costs, putting pressure on small and mid-sized businesses that could not easily adapt to price fluctuations.

The tariffs also strained relationships with traditional U.S. allies, including Canada, the European Union, and Japan, who were major suppliers of steel and aluminum. These countries retaliated with their own tariffs on American goods, escalating tensions and disrupting trade partnerships. Canada, for example, imposed countermeasures on U.S. exports such as whiskey, orange juice, and dairy products, creating economic ripple effects across multiple sectors. Critics of the tariffs argued that targeting allies made little sense from a national security perspective, as Canada and the EU were among the closest military and economic partners of the United States. Instead of isolating China, the tariffs alienated key allies and led to diplomatic disputes that complicated broader U.S. trade negotiations.

By the end of Trump's presidency, the long-term effectiveness of the steel and aluminum tariffs remained in question. While the tariffs had succeeded in temporarily boosting domestic production, they had also raised costs for manufacturers, disrupted supply chains, and triggered international retaliation. The debate over whether these tariffs genuinely strengthened national defense or simply created economic hardships continued, highlighting the complexity of using trade policy as a tool for security objectives.

Economic Independence vs. Global Cooperation

Donald Trump's tariff policies reignited the debate between economic independence and global cooperation, two competing approaches that have shaped U.S. trade policy for decades. The administration argued that tariffs and protectionist measures were necessary to reduce reliance on foreign goods, bring manufacturing jobs back to the United States, and protect national security. This vision of economic independence was framed as an effort to reclaim control over critical industries, ensuring that America could sustain itself without being at the mercy of international markets. However, the trade war and its consequences highlighted the challenges of pursuing self-sufficiency in an interconnected global economy, raising questions about whether complete economic independence is realistic or even beneficial in the modern era.

Trump's push for economic independence was rooted in the belief that globalization had harmed American workers, particularly in manufacturing and industrial sectors. His administration viewed free trade agreements and international supply chains as major contributors to job losses, as companies moved production overseas to take advantage of cheaper labor and resources. By imposing tariffs on Chinese imports, steel, aluminum, and other foreign goods, the goal was to make it more attractive for businesses to manufacture domestically. The administration also pressured corporations to reshore jobs and reduce reliance on foreign suppliers, arguing that a stronger domestic economy would enhance national security and economic resilience. Supporters of this approach pointed out that depending too much on foreign nations for critical goods, such as technology and medical supplies, posed risks, particularly in times of crisis or geopolitical tension.

However, the pursuit of economic independence clashed with the reality of global cooperation, which had defined international trade for decades. Modern economies are deeply intertwined, with supply chains stretching across multiple continents, allowing businesses to source materials and components efficiently and affordably. The trade war disrupted these supply chains, making it clear that cutting off access to international markets came with significant costs. Companies faced higher prices for raw materials and production delays, as finding domestic alternatives was often impractical or too expensive. Industries such as automotive, technology, and agriculture struggled to adjust, as their operations had been built around global trade partnerships that could not be easily dismantled.

The impact of tariffs also extended to America's diplomatic and economic relationships with key allies. Traditional U.S. partners, such as Canada, Mexico, and the European Union, pushed back against Trump's protectionist policies, retaliating with their own tariffs on American goods. Instead of strengthening U.S. economic power, the trade war isolated the country in many global trade discussions, as other nations pursued new agreements without American involvement. China, the European Union, and Pacific nations strengthened their trade ties, making the U.S. less central to global commerce. Many businesses and policymakers questioned whether economic independence was worth the cost of alienating trading partners and increasing costs for domestic industries.

By the end of Trump's presidency, the trade war had demonstrated the challenges of balancing economic independence with global cooperation. While tariffs encouraged some domestic investment, they also created inflationary pressures, disrupted industries, and weakened diplomatic ties. The long-term lesson from the trade war was that while economic self-sufficiency is an appealing concept, true prosperity often depends on a balance between protecting domestic interests and engaging in strategic global cooperation.

The Role of Tariffs in Cybersecurity and Technology

The Trump administration's use of tariffs extended beyond traditional industries like manufacturing and agriculture to the critical sectors of cybersecurity and technology, areas that play a vital role in both national security and economic competitiveness. The trade war with China was not just about balancing trade deficits—it was also a response to growing concerns about intellectual property theft, cybersecurity vulnerabilities, and China's dominance in key technological industries such as 5G, artificial intelligence (AI), and semiconductor production. Tariffs and trade restrictions were used as tools to limit China's access to American technology while encouraging the domestic development of critical infrastructure. However, these policies also had unintended consequences, disrupting global supply chains, increasing costs for American companies, and raising concerns about the long-term effectiveness of tariffs in addressing cybersecurity threats.

One of the most significant targets of the trade war was China's telecommunications giant Huawei, which had become a leader in 5G technology. The Trump administration viewed Huawei as a national security threat, alleging that its equipment could be used by the Chinese government for espionage and cyberattacks. In response, the U.S. imposed strict trade restrictions on Huawei, banning American companies from selling components, software, and services to the company without government approval. This move effectively cut Huawei off from key suppliers, including Google, Qualcomm, and Intel, making it difficult for the company to maintain its competitive edge. While the administration argued that these measures were necessary to protect U.S. cybersecurity and prevent potential backdoor surveillance, the restrictions also hurt American tech firms that relied on Chinese markets for revenue. Companies like Apple, Microsoft, and semiconductor manufacturers faced retaliatory actions from China, further escalating trade tensions.

Beyond specific companies, tariffs were also used to reduce U.S. dependence on Chinese-made technology components. Many American industries, including telecommunications, consumer electronics, and defense, rely on Chinese-manufactured semiconductors, circuit boards, and rare earth minerals—materials essential for the production of high-tech goods. The administration sought to incentivize domestic chip production by imposing tariffs on Chinese electronic components while investing in U.S. semiconductor manufacturing. However, shifting semiconductor production away from China proved challenging, as American companies had spent decades building global supply chains to maximize efficiency and reduce costs. As a result, tariffs led to increased costs for tech firms, forcing some companies to pass those costs onto consumers or look for alternative suppliers in Vietnam, Taiwan, and South Korea.

Despite the administration's efforts to use tariffs as a tool for cybersecurity and technological self-sufficiency, the effectiveness of this strategy remained debated. While some progress was made in reducing dependence on Chinese technology, the trade war also created disruptions in innovation, increased prices for American consumers, and damaged international trade relationships. China responded by accelerating its own technological independence efforts, investing heavily in domestic semiconductor production and AI development to counteract U.S. restrictions. The unintended consequence of tariffs was that instead of weakening China's technological dominance, they pushed Beijing to become more self-reliant, potentially making future competition even more intense. In the long run, the role of tariffs in cybersecurity and technology highlighted the complex relationship between national security, economic policy, and global innovation, leaving policymakers with the challenge of balancing protectionism with maintaining a leading role in the global tech economy.

Energy and Resource Dependence: A Balancing Act

The Trump administration's trade policies not only targeted manufacturing and technology but also played a significant role in shaping America's energy and resource dependence. Tariffs were used as a tool to reduce reliance on foreign energy sources and critical raw materials, while simultaneously encouraging domestic production and resource independence. However, this approach created both opportunities and challenges, as the U.S. attempted to balance its energy security, trade relations, and economic competitiveness. The result was a complex balancing act, where tariffs aimed at strengthening domestic industries also led to higher costs, supply chain disruptions, and diplomatic tensions with key trading partners.

One of the key areas affected by the trade war was the energy sector, particularly in relation to oil, natural gas, and renewable energy components. The U.S. had become a leading exporter of crude oil and liquefied natural gas (LNG), and China was one of its largest buyers. However, in retaliation for Trump's tariffs, China imposed its own tariffs on American oil and LNG, leading to a decline in U.S. energy exports to one of the world's biggest markets. This shift forced American energy companies to seek alternative buyers, increasing trade with Europe and other Asian nations but at less favorable terms. The impact of tariffs also extended to the renewable energy sector, as the U.S. imposed duties on imported solar panels and wind turbine components, many of which came from China. While this was intended to protect American solar and wind manufacturers, it had the unintended effect of raising costs for domestic energy projects, slowing down the transition to renewable energy.

Beyond energy, the trade war also highlighted America's dependence on critical raw materials, particularly rare earth minerals, which are essential for producing electronics, defense equipment, and clean energy technologies. China dominates the global supply of rare earths, and Trump's tariffs on Chinese goods raised concerns about whether the U.S. could secure a stable supply of these essential materials. In response, the administration sought to reduce reliance on Chinese rare earths by encouraging domestic mining and partnerships with alternative suppliers such as Australia and Canada. However, developing new mining operations is a long-term process, and in the short term, U.S. manufacturers faced higher costs and supply chain disruptions. The tariffs also led to increased investment in recycling and alternative materials, as industries sought ways to lessen their exposure to geopolitical trade risks.

The broader impact of tariffs on energy and resource dependence revealed the trade-offs between economic protectionism and global integration. While some domestic industries benefited from reduced foreign competition, the overall effect was higher costs, strained trade relationships, and a more uncertain supply chain for essential materials. Energy producers had to navigate new trade dynamics, while manufacturers faced the challenge of securing critical resources at competitive prices. The pursuit of energy and resource independence remained an important goal, but the trade war demonstrated that achieving it required more than just tariffs—it required strategic planning, investment in domestic capabilities, and stronger alliances with reliable trade partners. The challenge moving forward was to find a way to balance national security concerns with economic realities, ensuring that the U.S. remained competitive in an increasingly interconnected global market.

Chapter 6
Trump vs. Biden: A Tariff Policy Comparison

Donald Trump's trade policies, particularly his use of tariffs as a central economic strategy, marked a significant shift in U.S. trade relations. His administration took a protectionist approach, imposing tariffs on key imports from China, the European Union, Canada, and Mexico, arguing that these measures were necessary to protect American industries, reduce trade deficits, and strengthen national security. The tariffs led to trade wars, retaliatory measures from other nations, and economic uncertainty, with mixed results. While some domestic industries saw temporary gains, others, particularly those reliant on global supply chains, faced higher costs and business disruptions. Trump's strategy represented a fundamental departure from the free trade policies of previous administrations, favoring a more aggressive and unilateral approach to global trade.

When Joe Biden took office in 2021, many expected a dramatic shift in trade policy, with hopes that he would roll back Trump's tariffs and restore more traditional trade relationships. However, Biden's administration largely maintained many of the tariffs imposed by Trump, particularly those targeting China. Rather than immediately reversing Trump's trade policies, Biden took a more diplomatic and strategic approach, seeking to negotiate trade agreements with allies while continuing to use tariffs as leverage. His administration focused on strengthening alliances, working within multilateral frameworks like the G7 and WTO, and investing in domestic production to reduce dependency on foreign goods. The key difference between the two administrations was that while Trump used tariffs as a tool for economic confrontation, Biden used them as part of a broader strategy to reshape supply chains and strengthen U.S. economic resilience.

The comparison between Trump and Biden's tariff policies highlights the evolving nature of U.S. trade strategy in response to shifting global dynamics. While Trump's tariffs were bold, unpredictable, and unilateral, Biden's approach has been more calculated, focusing on long-term competitiveness rather than immediate trade wars. The debate over tariffs remains ongoing, with some arguing that Trump's aggressive stance forced necessary changes in global trade, while others believe that Biden's emphasis on alliances and economic security offers a more sustainable path forward. Ultimately, the question remains whether tariffs should remain a core component of U.S. trade policy or whether alternative strategies, such as diplomatic trade negotiations and domestic investment, will prove more effective in the long run.

Trump's Tariff Strategy: A Long-Term Plan or Short-Term Gamble?

Donald Trump's tariff strategy was one of the most defining aspects of his economic policy, but the question remains: was it a long-term plan to reshape global trade, or was it a short-term gamble that created more economic disruption than lasting benefits? His administration positioned tariffs as a strategic tool to reduce trade deficits, encourage domestic manufacturing, and hold China accountable for what he called unfair trade practices. However, the implementation of these policies often appeared reactive rather than part of a well-structured long-term economic plan. While Trump argued that tariffs would force trading partners to make concessions, critics pointed out that the economic costs, market volatility, and retaliatory measures from other nations made it unclear whether the benefits outweighed the risks.

One of the key arguments for Trump's tariff strategy being a long-term economic shift was his administration's belief that decades of free trade had hollowed out American industries. By imposing tariffs on steel, aluminum, automobiles, and consumer goods, Trump aimed to create a more self-sufficient U.S. economy, reducing reliance on China, Mexico, and European imports. In this sense, tariffs were not just meant to be temporary trade measures, but part of a broader effort to reshape supply chains, encourage domestic investment, and force multinational corporations to rethink their global strategies. If successful, this shift could have redefined U.S. trade policy for decades, strengthening domestic industries and reducing vulnerabilities to global supply chain disruptions.

However, in practice, many of the effects of Trump's tariffs seemed to resemble a short-term gamble with high economic risks rather than a sustainable long-term strategy. While some industries, such as domestic steel and aluminum, saw an initial boost in production, the broader economic impact was less positive. Many manufacturers, particularly automakers, technology companies, and small businesses, struggled with rising costs of raw materials. Instead of reshoring production to the U.S., many companies moved their supply chains to other low-cost countries like Vietnam, India, and Mexico to avoid the tariffs. Meanwhile, China and the European Union responded with their own retaliatory tariffs, leading to a trade war that hurt American farmers and exporters. The lack of a clear long-term exit strategy for these trade disputes left many businesses uncertain about their future, discouraging new investments.

The timing and unpredictability of Trump's tariff announcements further fueled the perception that his trade strategy was more reactive than strategic. Market volatility surged each time new tariffs were imposed or when trade negotiations with China collapsed, leading to instability in the stock market and business planning. While Trump believed that economic pressure would force China and other countries to renegotiate trade agreements in America's favor, the reality was that these nations adapted to the new trade environment by forming new economic alliances and diversifying their supply chains.

By the end of Trump's presidency, many of the tariffs remained in place, but their effectiveness remained unclear. While his policies succeeded in shaking up global trade dynamics, they did not lead to a major reshoring of jobs or a significant reduction in the trade deficit. Instead, they left behind higher consumer prices, economic uncertainty, and strained international relationships. Whether Trump's tariffs were a bold economic transformation or a risky short-term gamble remains a subject of debate, but one thing is certain—they reshaped U.S. trade policy in ways that continue to have lasting consequences.

Biden's Approach: Repeal, Revise, or Reinforce?

Joe Biden's approach to tariffs and trade policy differed significantly from Donald Trump's, but rather than fully repealing Trump-era tariffs, his administration opted for a strategic mix of revision and reinforcement. While many expected Biden to immediately reverse Trump's tariffs upon taking office, the reality was more complex. His administration recognized that tariffs could serve as leverage in trade negotiations and as a tool to counter China's growing economic influence. Instead of completely dismantling Trump's trade policies, Biden took a measured approach, maintaining some tariffs while adjusting others to align with broader diplomatic and economic goals.

Rather than using tariffs as a unilateral economic weapon, Biden focused on multilateral cooperation and alliance-building, seeking to repair relationships with key trade partners such as Canada, the European Union, and Japan. His administration removed tariffs on steel and aluminum imports from allied nations, easing tensions with traditional allies while preserving tariffs on China, which was still seen as a strategic competitor. This approach allowed Biden to strengthen U.S. partnerships and counter China's influence collectively, rather than engaging in the unpredictable, tit-for-tat trade war that defined the Trump era. However, some critics argued that Biden's partial tariff reductions did not go far enough, as American businesses and consumers continued to face higher prices on goods impacted by lingering tariffs.

One of Biden's key trade strategies was investing in domestic industries rather than relying solely on tariffs to reshape global trade. His administration pushed forward policies such as the CHIPS and Science Act, which aimed to boost domestic semiconductor production, reducing dependence on Chinese and Taiwanese chip manufacturers. Biden also promoted "Made in America" policies, encouraging U.S. companies to invest in local supply chains instead of moving production overseas. Unlike Trump, who used tariffs as a primary tool to force companies to reshore jobs, Biden adopted a more incentive-driven approach, offering subsidies and tax credits to encourage domestic manufacturing growth. This shift represented a key difference: where Trump sought to punish companies for outsourcing, Biden aimed to reward companies for staying in the U.S.

Despite these strategic shifts, Biden's administration faced many of the same economic challenges as Trump's, particularly regarding inflation and supply chain disruptions. The COVID-19 pandemic and geopolitical tensions further complicated global trade, making it difficult to determine whether tariffs were helping or hurting the economy. While Biden sought to reduce dependence on China, the reality was that American businesses remained deeply integrated into global supply chains, making it difficult to rapidly shift production without causing economic disruptions. Additionally, China retaliated against continued U.S. trade restrictions, maintaining tensions between the two economic giants.

By the end of Biden's first term, his trade policy remained a blend of continuity and change. While he eased some tariffs and reinforced global alliances, he also maintained a tough stance on China and promoted domestic industry growth. The debate over whether Biden's approach was more effective than Trump's remained open, as businesses and policymakers continued to weigh the benefits of protectionism versus global trade cooperation. One thing was clear — Biden's tariff strategy was less about confrontation and more about strategic economic positioning, signaling a shift in how the U.S. engages in global trade moving forward.

Trade Relations with China: The Shifting Stance

The United States' trade relationship with China has been one of the most complex and evolving aspects of global economics, and the transition from Trump to Biden marked a shift in approach while maintaining a fundamentally cautious stance toward the world's second-largest economy. While Trump's aggressive trade war, centered around tariffs and economic pressure, sought to force China into economic concessions, Biden's administration adopted a more diplomatic yet firm approach, aiming to counter China's influence through multilateral alliances and domestic investment rather than unilateral trade battles. The key question remained: Would the shift in strategy lead to improved trade relations, or would tensions continue under a new framework?

Under Trump, the U.S.-China trade war escalated through a series of high tariffs, impacting hundreds of billions of dollars in traded goods. The Trump administration accused China of intellectual property theft, forced technology transfers, currency manipulation, and unfair trade practices. In response, it imposed tariffs on Chinese imports, aiming to reduce the U.S. trade deficit and encourage companies to move production away from China. While some American manufacturers did seek alternative supply chains, the overall impact of the tariffs was mixed, as many businesses struggled with higher production costs, supply chain disruptions, and retaliatory tariffs imposed by China. The Phase One trade deal, signed in early 2020, required China to increase purchases of American goods, including agricultural products, energy, and manufactured goods, but the deal's long-term effectiveness was uncertain.

When Biden took office, many expected him to immediately roll back Trump's tariffs and seek a new trade agreement with China, but his administration instead took a more measured approach. While Biden eased tensions with U.S. allies like the European Union and Canada, he largely maintained Trump's tough stance on China, keeping most tariffs in place while shifting focus to strategic competition rather than outright economic conflict. Instead of using tariffs as a primary tool, Biden sought to counterbalance China's influence by strengthening trade alliances with democratic nations, such as forming the Indo-Pacific Economic Framework (IPEF) to increase economic cooperation in Asia without direct confrontation. This approach aimed to reduce reliance on Chinese supply chains by encouraging diversification and investment in alternative manufacturing hubs like Vietnam, India, and Taiwan.

A key aspect of Biden's strategy was investing in domestic industries to lessen dependence on Chinese goods and technology. His administration passed the CHIPS and Science Act, providing billions of dollars in incentives for U.S.-based semiconductor production, a sector where China has sought dominance. Similarly, Biden tightened restrictions on China's access to advanced U.S. technology, particularly in areas like artificial intelligence, 5G infrastructure, and defense-related tech. These moves were seen as part of a broader strategy to limit China's economic and technological expansion without relying solely on tariffs.

Despite the differences in tactics, both Trump and Biden viewed China as a strategic rival, and the fundamental economic tensions between the two nations remained unresolved. While Biden's less confrontational, alliance-driven approach reduced some trade volatility, deep-rooted issues such as intellectual property disputes, human rights concerns, and geopolitical tensions in Taiwan and the South China Sea continued to make trade relations fragile. The future of U.S.-China trade remains uncertain, as both nations navigate the challenges of economic interdependence, technological competition, and shifting global power dynamics.

The Future of "America First" Economics

Donald Trump's "America First" economic policy reshaped U.S. trade and industrial strategy, focusing on protectionism, reshoring jobs, and reducing dependence on foreign markets. His administration championed tariffs, trade renegotiations, and economic nationalism as tools to protect American industries and workers. While this approach resonated with many who believed that globalization had hollowed out American manufacturing, it also sparked trade wars, price increases, and diplomatic tensions. As Trump left office and Biden took over, the question remained: Does "America First" have a long-term future, or will global economic realities push the U.S. back toward free trade and international cooperation?

One of the lasting impacts of "America First" economics has been a greater emphasis on domestic manufacturing and supply chain resilience. The COVID-19 pandemic further exposed America's reliance on foreign goods, particularly in medical supplies, semiconductors, and energy resources, reinforcing the idea that the U.S. must strengthen its domestic production capabilities. Biden, despite his more multilateral approach, has continued certain elements of Trump's protectionist policies, maintaining tariffs on China, restricting technology exports, and promoting government investments in key industries. This suggests that economic nationalism did not leave with Trump—instead, it evolved into a more strategic, long-term plan to counter economic vulnerabilities while balancing global partnerships.

However, the future of "America First" economics faces significant challenges, particularly as businesses and industries remain deeply intertwined with global trade networks. Many companies that initially relocated supply chains to avoid tariffs found it difficult to fully disengage from China and other low-cost production hubs. Additionally, tariffs and trade barriers raised costs for American consumers and businesses, creating economic friction that some argue hurt the U.S. economy more than it helped. The shift toward regionalization rather than full economic independence has become more apparent, with American companies diversifying production across multiple countries rather than returning all operations to U.S. soil.

Another factor shaping the future of "America First" policies is the geopolitical landscape. The rise of China as an economic powerhouse, tensions in the South China Sea, and Russia's global influence have reinforced the belief that economic strength is linked to national security. As a result, policies that encourage domestic innovation, reduce reliance on geopolitical rivals, and invest in American industries will likely remain a priority, regardless of political leadership. The Biden administration's focus on semiconductors, clean energy, and infrastructure investment mirrors some of Trump's economic goals, but with a greater emphasis on strategic alliances rather than unilateral trade battles.

The long-term survival of "America First" economics will depend on how well it adapts to the realities of globalization. While self-sufficiency and domestic job growth remain appealing, completely isolating the U.S. from international trade is neither practical nor economically viable. Instead, a hybrid approach—one that protects critical industries while maintaining beneficial global trade relationships—is likely to emerge as the dominant model. The core idea of prioritizing American workers and industries will persist, but future administrations will need to balance economic nationalism with the benefits of international cooperation, ensuring that "America First" does not become America alone.

Chapter 7
Lessons from the Trade War

The U.S.-China trade war, initiated under Donald Trump's administration, was one of the most significant economic conflicts in recent history, reshaping global trade policies and influencing economic strategies worldwide. While the Trump administration framed tariffs as a tool to correct trade imbalances, protect American industries, and challenge China's economic dominance, the long-term effects of these policies have been widely debated. Some industries benefited from tariff protections, while others struggled with increased costs, supply chain disruptions, and market uncertainty. As the dust settled, policymakers, businesses, and economists were left with valuable lessons about the effectiveness, limitations, and unintended consequences of trade wars.

One of the biggest takeaways from the trade war was that tariffs are not a simple solution for complex economic issues. While Trump's administration believed that tariffs would force China into making economic concessions, the reality was that both countries suffered economic setbacks, and China adapted by diversifying its trade partnerships. The retaliatory tariffs imposed by China hurt American farmers and exporters, leading to billions of dollars in government subsidies to mitigate their losses. Meanwhile, businesses reliant on global supply chains faced higher production costs, which were ultimately passed down to American consumers. This demonstrated that trade wars are rarely "easy to win" and can lead to long-term economic instability rather than quick victories.

Another critical lesson was the importance of strategic alliances and trade diversification in navigating global economic challenges. While Trump's approach was largely unilateral, focusing on direct confrontations with China, many businesses and policymakers realized that strengthening trade relationships with allies could provide better economic security. Countries like Vietnam, India, and Mexico became alternative manufacturing hubs, showing that companies will seek the most cost-effective solutions rather than simply reshoring to the U.S.. Additionally, the trade war highlighted the need for domestic investment in critical industries, such as semiconductor production and rare earth minerals, to reduce reliance on foreign suppliers. As the U.S. moves forward, the lessons from the trade war will continue to shape trade policies, economic strategies, and global partnerships for years to come.

Did Tariffs Work? Measuring Success and Failure

The effectiveness of Donald Trump's tariffs remains one of the most debated aspects of his economic policy. His administration argued that tariffs would protect American industries, reduce trade deficits, and force China and other countries to negotiate fairer trade agreements. However, the actual results of the trade war were mixed, with some industries seeing short-term benefits while others experienced increased costs, job losses, and economic instability. By examining key economic indicators such as trade deficits, job growth, consumer prices, and industrial output, we can better assess whether the tariffs achieved their intended goals or if they ended up hurting the very people they were meant to protect.

One of the primary justifications for the tariffs was to reduce the U.S. trade deficit, particularly with China. The idea was that by making Chinese imports more expensive, American companies and consumers would buy more domestically produced goods, leading to a narrowing of the trade gap. However, the trade deficit with China remained high throughout Trump's presidency, with only minor fluctuations. While imports from China declined, American companies did not shift entirely to U.S.-made products—instead, they turned to alternative suppliers in countries like Vietnam, India, and Mexico. This indicated that tariffs did not fundamentally change trade imbalances, but rather redirected supply chains without significantly boosting American manufacturing.

Another goal of the tariffs was to create jobs in American industries that had been affected by globalization, particularly in manufacturing, steel, and aluminum. While some domestic steel producers benefited in the short term, the overall impact on jobs was negative due to higher production costs for industries reliant on imported materials. Automakers, construction companies, and technology firms faced increased costs for steel, aluminum, and electronic components, leading to layoffs, production slowdowns, and higher consumer prices. General Motors and Ford, for example, reported billions in increased costs due to tariffs, resulting in plant closures and job cuts instead of job growth. The agricultural sector also suffered, as China's retaliatory tariffs crippled American farmers, leading to lost export markets and billions in government bailout subsidies to offset their losses.

The impact on consumers was another key measure of success or failure. The tariffs led to higher prices on everyday goods, from household appliances and electronics to cars and food products. The Federal Reserve Bank of New York estimated that the trade war cost the average American household around $1,200 per year due to rising costs. This undermined one of Trump's main promises—to help working-class Americans—as middle- and low-income families were hit hardest by these price increases. Instead of making American-made products more competitive, the tariffs often forced businesses to raise prices, cut jobs, or find more expensive workarounds.

While Trump's tariffs did bring attention to issues such as China's trade practices and the need for supply chain diversification, they ultimately failed to deliver lasting economic gains. Instead of reviving American manufacturing, the trade war caused economic uncertainty, disrupted supply chains, and strained relationships with key allies. In the end, the tariffs did not fundamentally reshape global trade in America's favor but rather exposed the risks of aggressive protectionist policies without a clear long-term strategy.

Economic Sovereignty vs. Economic Burden

The debate over economic sovereignty versus economic burden has been at the heart of U.S. trade policy, particularly under Donald Trump's administration. His tariffs were introduced as a way to restore economic independence, reduce reliance on foreign goods, and protect American industries, reinforcing the idea of economic sovereignty. The administration argued that by imposing tariffs on imports, particularly from China, the U.S. could reclaim control over manufacturing, technology, and critical supply chains, reducing vulnerabilities associated with globalization. However, while the concept of economic sovereignty is appealing, the reality was more complicated. The tariffs created higher costs for businesses and consumers, supply chain disruptions, and retaliatory trade restrictions, leading many to question whether the policy strengthened the U.S. economy or simply became an economic burden.

One of the core principles of economic sovereignty is self-sufficiency, ensuring that key industries, especially those related to national security and essential goods, are not dependent on foreign nations. Trump's tariffs on steel, aluminum, and technology components were meant to revitalize domestic manufacturing and encourage companies to reshore jobs that had been outsourced to countries with lower labor costs. In theory, this would lead to a stronger domestic industrial base, reduced trade deficits, and increased economic resilience in times of global uncertainty. The COVID-19 pandemic later reinforced the importance of this approach, as supply chain disruptions made clear how dependent the U.S. had become on foreign suppliers for medical equipment, semiconductors, and other critical goods. The argument for economic sovereignty gained traction as policymakers realized that certain dependencies could pose security risks and should be addressed through domestic production and investment.

However, achieving economic sovereignty came with significant economic burdens, especially for industries that relied on imported raw materials and global supply chains. When tariffs raised the price of steel, aluminum, and Chinese-made components, companies in automotive, construction, technology, and consumer goods sectors faced rising production costs, forcing them to raise prices, cut jobs, or shift supply chains to alternative foreign markets like Vietnam and India rather than bringing them back to the U.S. For many businesses, the tariffs increased costs without creating clear domestic alternatives, leading to uncertainty and financial strain. Instead of a full reshoring of industries, the trade war caused disruptions in global commerce, making it harder for businesses to plan for long-term investments.

Consumers also bore the economic burden of tariffs, as companies passed on higher costs to customers. Prices for household appliances, cars, electronics, and even groceries increased due to the cost of imported goods rising under the tariff policies. A study by the Federal Reserve Bank of New York estimated that the trade war cost the average American household over $1,200 per year in additional expenses. This contradicted the promise that tariffs would benefit working-class Americans, as everyday necessities became more expensive, lowering purchasing power and contributing to inflation.

The trade-off between economic sovereignty and economic burden remains a key issue in U.S. trade policy. While ensuring that the U.S. is not overly dependent on foreign nations for critical goods is essential, the costs of aggressive protectionist policies need to be weighed against the long-term economic impact. The lesson from Trump's trade war is that achieving true economic independence requires more than just tariffs—it requires strategic investments in domestic industries, supply chain diversification, and stronger trade partnerships to balance sovereignty with economic growth.

The Role of Diplomacy in Trade Policy

The role of diplomacy in trade policy is crucial in shaping economic relationships, resolving disputes, and fostering global cooperation. While trade wars and tariffs can be used as economic weapons, diplomacy serves as a more sustainable tool for negotiating fair trade agreements, strengthening alliances, and ensuring economic stability. The contrast between Donald Trump's aggressive, unilateral approach and Joe Biden's more diplomatic, alliance-driven strategy highlights how different trade policies can impact the U.S.

economy and its global standing. While Trump's administration relied heavily on tariffs, threats, and economic confrontation, Biden sought to restore partnerships and work within multilateral frameworks to address trade imbalances and security concerns. This shift demonstrated that while economic pressure can yield short-term results, diplomacy is often essential for long-term success in trade relations.

Trump's trade policy was largely defined by unilateral actions, such as imposing steep tariffs on China, the European Union, Canada, and Mexico, without prior negotiations. The goal was to force trading partners into concessions and push for bilateral trade agreements that prioritized American interests. However, this approach often led to retaliatory tariffs, diplomatic tensions, and economic uncertainty. Traditional allies, such as Canada and the European Union, responded with their own trade restrictions, leading to strained relationships that impacted industries on both sides. While the Phase One trade deal with China was seen as a diplomatic victory, it did not resolve long-term structural issues such as intellectual property theft and market access, showing the limitations of a purely confrontational approach. The trade war resulted in billions of dollars in losses for American farmers and businesses, forcing the U.S. government to issue subsidies to offset damages, which could have been avoided through negotiation and strategic cooperation.

Biden's administration took a different approach, emphasizing multilateral trade diplomacy and strategic economic partnerships. Instead of escalating trade conflicts, Biden eased tariffs on key allies, such as lifting steel and aluminum tariffs on the EU and Canada, which helped restore trust and rebuild trade relationships. His administration focused on collaborating with partners like the G7, the European Union, and Indo-Pacific nations to create a united front against China's economic influence. Rather than relying solely on tariffs, Biden's trade policy included domestic investment strategies, such as the CHIPS and Science Act, which aimed to strengthen domestic semiconductor production and reduce dependence on Chinese technology. By working within diplomatic frameworks, the Biden administration sought to balance national security concerns with economic growth, demonstrating the importance of diplomacy in achieving long-term trade stability.

The effectiveness of diplomacy in trade policy is evident in how strong trade agreements and alliances create economic resilience. Multilateral agreements, such as the Comprehensive and Progressive Agreement for Trans-Pacific Partnership (CPTPP) and the United States-Mexico-Canada Agreement (USMCA), show how diplomacy can create mutually beneficial trade rules that enhance market access and reduce reliance on tariffs and economic coercion. While Trump's tariffs disrupted global supply chains, Biden's diplomatic approach aimed to create new trade opportunities without unnecessary economic conflict. Ultimately, diplomacy in trade policy is not just about avoiding tariffs—it is about creating a stable economic environment, fostering innovation, and ensuring that U.S. businesses remain competitive in a rapidly changing global economy.

The Road Ahead: Tariffs or Free Trade?

The debate over tariffs versus free trade remains central to the future of U.S. economic policy. While tariffs are often seen as a way to protect domestic industries, address trade imbalances, and counter unfair practices by foreign governments, free trade is viewed as a driver of economic growth, innovation, and lower costs for businesses and consumers. The Trump administration's heavy reliance on tariffs highlighted both the potential benefits and unintended consequences of protectionist policies, while the Biden administration's approach has sought to balance domestic industry support with international cooperation. As the U.S. moves forward, policymakers must weigh the short-term gains of tariffs against the long-term advantages of open trade agreements, determining the best course for economic stability and competitiveness in a rapidly evolving global landscape.

Tariffs have historically been used to shield domestic industries from foreign competition, and in some cases, they have succeeded in boosting local production and protecting jobs. Trump's tariffs on steel, aluminum, and Chinese imports were meant to reduce dependency on foreign goods and encourage American companies to bring manufacturing back to the U.S. While some domestic industries saw temporary benefits, many others faced higher costs for imported materials, supply chain disruptions, and retaliatory tariffs from trade partners. The economic burden of tariffs often fell on businesses and consumers, leading to higher prices for goods, reduced exports, and financial strain on key industries like agriculture and automotive manufacturing. The trade war with China, in particular, highlighted the risks of relying too heavily on tariffs, as it led to billions in economic losses without achieving a decisive victory in trade negotiations.

Free trade, on the other hand, has long been seen as a catalyst for global economic expansion, enabling businesses to access new markets, lower costs, and drive innovation. Trade agreements such as NAFTA (now USMCA) and the Trans-Pacific Partnership (TPP) were designed to facilitate seamless trade across borders, reducing tariffs and encouraging investment. The benefits of free trade include greater consumer choice, increased competition leading to better products, and expanded opportunities for American businesses to sell abroad. However, critics argue that unregulated free trade can harm domestic industries, encourage outsourcing, and create dependence on foreign manufacturing, particularly in sectors critical to national security, technology, and energy. The challenge is finding a balanced approach that protects American interests while maintaining economic openness.

The road ahead will likely see a hybrid approach, blending elements of tariffs and strategic free trade policies to create a more resilient and self-sufficient economy. Biden's focus on strengthening domestic industries through incentives rather than punitive tariffs suggests a shift toward economic security through investment rather than confrontation. However, competition with China, supply chain vulnerabilities, and the need for energy independence may keep tariffs as a useful policy tool in specific industries. Moving forward, the U.S. must consider whether to engage more in multilateral trade agreements, protect key industries through targeted tariffs, or find alternative solutions that balance economic growth with security concerns. The future of trade policy will depend on navigating these complexities while ensuring that U.S. businesses remain competitive in a rapidly changing global economy.

Chapter 8
The Political and Public Response to Tariffs

The political and public response to Donald Trump's tariffs was deeply divided, reflecting broader ideological differences about trade, economic nationalism, and global cooperation. While some politicians and voters embraced tariffs as a necessary tool to protect American jobs and industries, others viewed them as a burden on businesses and consumers that ultimately hurt the economy. The Trump administration argued that tariffs would level the playing field, reduce trade deficits, and encourage domestic manufacturing, but critics—including some within his own party—warned of retaliatory measures from trade partners, increased production costs, and economic uncertainty. The debate over tariffs quickly became a major political issue, shaping discussions in Congress, business circles, and among the general public.

The business community played a significant role in shaping the public response to tariffs, with reactions varying across industries. Steel and aluminum manufacturers initially benefited, as tariffs provided them with a competitive advantage over foreign imports. However, industries that relied on these raw materials—such as automotive, construction, and consumer goods manufacturers—faced higher costs, leading to job losses and higher prices for consumers. Retailers, farmers, and small business owners were among the hardest hit, as rising costs and supply chain disruptions forced many to absorb financial losses. Corporate lobbying efforts intensified, with some companies pushing for exemptions and trade negotiations, while others urged the government to roll back tariffs to avoid further economic harm.

Among voters, tariffs were a polarizing issue, with opinions largely influenced by economic circumstances and political affiliations. Many blue-collar workers and manufacturing employees saw tariffs as a step toward reviving American industry, reinforcing Trump's message of "America First" economic nationalism. However, farmers—particularly in the Midwest—felt betrayed as retaliatory tariffs from China crippled their ability to export soybeans, pork, and other agricultural products. The broader public, including consumers, faced rising prices on everyday goods, leading to concerns about inflation and the overall economic impact of the trade war. As the debate over tariffs unfolded, it became clear that while some groups stood to benefit, many others bore the economic burden—making tariffs a key political and economic battleground in the years that followed.

Congress and Trade Policy: Supporters vs. Critics

The debate over tariffs in Congress reflected a deep political and economic divide in U.S. trade policy. While some lawmakers supported Trump's aggressive use of tariffs as a tool to protect American jobs and industries, others criticized the approach as short-sighted, harmful to businesses, and detrimental to global trade relations. The Republican Party itself was divided, with some embracing Trump's economic nationalism and others maintaining traditional conservative support for free trade. Meanwhile, Democrats also took varied positions, with some arguing that tariffs were needed to counter China's unfair trade practices, while others believed they were damaging to American workers and consumers. The battle over tariffs in Congress highlighted the broader ideological shift in both parties, as economic nationalism clashed with global economic integration.

Many Republican lawmakers, particularly those aligned with Trump's "America First" agenda, supported tariffs as a means of protecting U.S. industries from foreign competition. They argued that for decades, free trade agreements had led to outsourcing, factory closures, and the decline of domestic manufacturing, leaving the U.S. economy vulnerable. Senators like Josh Hawley and Tom Cotton defended tariffs as a way to counter China's economic influence, safeguard national security, and reduce reliance on foreign supply chains. Additionally, lawmakers from industrial and manufacturing-heavy states backed the tariffs, believing they would lead to job growth in sectors like steel, aluminum, and automotive production. Some Democrats also supported tariffs, but for different reasons. Progressives such as Senator Bernie Sanders and Senator Sherrod Brown saw tariffs as a way to protect American workers from globalization, advocating for stronger labor protections alongside trade restrictions. They argued that corporate offshoring had devastated middle-class jobs and that tariffs could be used as leverage to negotiate better trade deals that prioritize American labor. This rare bipartisan alignment—between Trump's Republican supporters and certain left-wing Democrats—reflected the growing dissatisfaction with globalization and its impact on American workers.

Despite strong support from some sectors, many Republicans and Democrats opposed tariffs, warning of higher costs for businesses and consumers, supply chain disruptions, and retaliatory trade measures. Traditional conservative Republicans, including Senate Minority Leader Mitch McConnell and Senator Pat Toomey, expressed concern that tariffs contradicted the party's long-standing support for free markets. They argued that instead of boosting the economy, tariffs acted as a tax on American businesses, making production more expensive and ultimately leading to higher prices for consumers. Democratic critics, including Senator Elizabeth Warren and House Speaker Nancy Pelosi, focused on the negative economic consequences of the trade war, particularly on farmers and small businesses. Many pointed to the economic burden caused by China's retaliatory tariffs, which severely hurt American soybean farmers, pork producers, and other agricultural exporters. Some Democrats also criticized Trump for failing to negotiate effectively with China, arguing that his administration's unilateral tariffs alienated U.S. allies instead of building a united front against unfair Chinese trade practices.

The split in Congress led to heated debates and legislative efforts to modify trade policy. Some lawmakers pushed for Congressional oversight on tariffs, introducing bills to limit the president's ability to impose tariffs without approval from Congress. Others advocated for new trade agreements that balanced protectionist policies with economic cooperation, ensuring that tariffs did not escalate into prolonged trade wars. As the Biden administration took office, Congress continued to debate the future of tariffs, with some advocating for their removal and others pushing for a more strategic approach to trade restrictions. Ultimately, the battle over tariffs in Congress highlighted the deep tensions within U.S. trade policy. While economic nationalism gained traction, the reality of global economic interdependence made long-term protectionist policies difficult to sustain. Moving forward, lawmakers will need to find a balance between protecting American industries and maintaining strong international trade relationships, ensuring that future trade policies serve both economic and strategic national interests.

The Business Community: Corporate Reactions and Lobbying Efforts

The business community had a complex and often divided reaction to Donald Trump's tariff policies. While some industries, particularly those in domestic steel and aluminum production, welcomed protectionist measures that shielded them from foreign competition, others faced higher costs, disrupted supply chains, and decreased international competitiveness. The tariffs forced many corporations to reevaluate their global operations, with some passing increased costs onto consumers, others seeking alternative suppliers, and many engaging in lobbying efforts to influence trade policy. The corporate response to tariffs demonstrated the high stakes of trade policy and how businesses, regardless of size, had to navigate an uncertain economic landscape shaped by government intervention.

Large multinational corporations, particularly those reliant on global supply chains, were among the most vocal opponents of tariffs. Companies in the automotive, technology, and consumer goods sectors faced higher production costs due to increased prices for imported steel, aluminum, and electronic components. Automakers like Ford and General Motors publicly stated that tariffs were adding billions of dollars in additional costs, leading to job cuts and plant closures. The technology sector also suffered, with companies like Apple and Dell warning that tariffs on Chinese-made electronic components would make their products more expensive for American consumers. Retail giants such as Walmart and Target also voiced concerns, as tariffs on Chinese imports meant higher prices for everyday goods like clothing, appliances, and electronics. The impact on these companies underscored how interconnected modern supply chains had become and how tariffs had far-reaching consequences beyond just the industries they targeted.

While some businesses struggled, others benefited from tariffs, particularly those in the domestic steel, aluminum, and agricultural processing industries. U.S. steel manufacturers saw increased demand for their products, as tariffs on foreign steel made domestic options more competitive. Companies like U.S. Steel and Nucor Corporation reported short-term gains, as the tariffs protected them from cheap foreign imports, particularly from China. Similarly, some small manufacturers who had previously struggled to compete with low-cost foreign alternatives saw a revival in demand for domestically made products. However, these benefits were not evenly distributed, and for every company that profited from tariffs, many others faced economic challenges and increased operational costs.

Recognizing the significant impact of tariffs, business lobbying efforts intensified, with corporations and trade associations actively working to influence U.S. trade policy. Organizations like the U.S. Chamber of Commerce, the National Retail Federation, and the Business Roundtable lobbied against tariffs, arguing that they were harming American businesses and consumers. These groups called for more strategic trade policies rather than broad-based tariffs, pushing for diplomatic negotiations instead of prolonged trade wars. Some industries sought exemptions from tariffs, with varying levels of success, as the Trump administration granted waivers to certain companies while denying others. Businesses also pressured Congress to intervene, advocating for policies that would ease trade tensions while maintaining fair competition.

Ultimately, the business community's response to tariffs highlighted the complexity of modern trade policy, where protectionist measures could benefit some industries while simultaneously harming others. While Trump's tariffs were meant to revive American manufacturing, they also created new economic challenges, forcing businesses to adapt, lobby, and restructure their supply chains. The long-term effects of these policies continued to influence corporate decision-making, as companies weighed the risks of government intervention in trade against the realities of competing in a globalized economy.

Voter Perspectives: Economic Nationalism vs. Economic Reality

The debate over tariffs and trade policy during the Trump administration sparked divided opinions among American voters, particularly in the context of economic nationalism versus economic reality. Many of Trump's supporters embraced tariffs as a necessary tool to restore American industry, protect jobs, and reduce dependence on foreign economies, particularly China. This perspective resonated strongly with blue-collar workers, manufacturing employees, and rural communities that had experienced job losses due to outsourcing and factory closures over previous decades. To them, Trump's tariffs represented a long-overdue pushback against globalization and a chance to reclaim economic sovereignty. However, as tariffs took effect, the economic reality proved more complicated, as rising costs, retaliatory trade measures, and supply chain disruptions led many to question whether tariffs were actually benefiting American workers and consumers.

Among Trump's core supporters, economic nationalism was a powerful political message that reinforced the idea that global trade deals had hurt American workers by prioritizing international corporations over domestic job security. Many working-class voters in industrial states like Michigan, Pennsylvania, and Ohio supported tariffs, believing they would revitalize manufacturing, encourage companies to reshore jobs, and reduce reliance on foreign imports. Trump's rhetoric about China's unfair trade practices, currency manipulation, and intellectual property theft also appealed to those who felt that previous administrations had failed to protect American interests. In states where factories had shut down due to cheaper foreign labor, voters saw tariffs as a bold action to reverse years of economic decline. Even if tariffs led to short-term economic pain, many voters believed they were a necessary step toward long-term economic independence.

However, as tariffs took effect, their consequences directly impacted many American households, especially those in industries dependent on international trade. Farmers in the Midwest and South, many of whom were traditionally Republican voters, faced devastating losses when China retaliated with tariffs on American agricultural exports. Soybean farmers, pork producers, and dairy farmers saw their biggest foreign market disappear overnight, leading to massive revenue losses. While the Trump administration attempted to offset these losses with government subsidies, many farmers still struggled with financial uncertainty and mounting debt. Some began to question whether economic nationalism was worth the trade war's cost, as they had been promised expanded markets but instead faced economic instability and reduced global demand.

Consumers also felt the financial strain of tariffs, particularly as the cost of imported goods rose. Everyday products, including electronics, appliances, clothing, and cars, became more expensive as companies passed increased import costs onto consumers. Lower-income and middle-class families, who often had less financial flexibility, were hit the hardest by these price hikes. While some still supported Trump's broader vision of economic nationalism, others became frustrated with the direct impact on their wallets. Some independent and moderate voters who had supported Trump's 2016 campaign began to reassess their views on tariffs, as the economic consequences of the trade war became more apparent.

Ultimately, the voter response to tariffs highlighted a deep ideological divide in how Americans viewed trade policy. While economic nationalism appealed to those seeking domestic industry revival and job security, the economic reality of higher costs, lost exports, and retaliatory measures challenged the notion that tariffs were an effective long-term strategy. This divide played a crucial role in shaping political debates in the 2020 election, as voters weighed the symbolic appeal of economic nationalism against the practical consequences of the trade war on their daily lives.

Media Narratives and Public Perception

The media played a crucial role in shaping public perception of Donald Trump's tariff policies, framing the trade war in different ways depending on political leanings, economic analysis, and industry impacts. Coverage varied significantly between news outlets, with some portraying tariffs as a bold, necessary move to protect American jobs and industries, while others highlighted the economic hardships, rising consumer costs, and diplomatic tensions caused by the trade war. As tariffs became a defining aspect of Trump's economic strategy, media narratives influenced how the public understood the impact of these policies, shaping both voter attitudes and broader economic debates.

Conservative-leaning media, such as Fox News and right-wing commentators, largely framed tariffs as a strategic move to counter China's economic aggression and restore American manufacturing. They echoed Trump's messaging that the U.S. had been taken advantage of for decades, and that tariffs were a long-overdue corrective measure to balance trade deficits and reclaim economic sovereignty. These outlets often emphasized the short-term sacrifices required for long-term economic strength, portraying farmers, manufacturers, and consumers who experienced financial strain as patriots enduring temporary hardship for the greater good. Reports focused on job creation in certain protected industries, particularly domestic steel and aluminum production, reinforcing the narrative that tariffs were delivering results despite broader economic concerns.

Liberal-leaning media, including CNN, MSNBC, The New York Times, and The Washington Post, took a more critical stance, emphasizing the economic downsides and global instability caused by the tariffs. These outlets focused on the rising costs of goods, job losses in industries reliant on global supply chains, and the negative effects on farmers due to retaliatory tariffs from China. Coverage frequently included interviews with struggling business owners and consumers, highlighting how tariffs were acting as a tax on American households rather than punishing foreign governments. Critics in the media also questioned Trump's negotiating tactics, arguing that unilateral tariffs alienated U.S. allies and weakened American influence in global trade negotiations. Rather than seeing tariffs as a strategic economic shift, liberal media often framed them as reactionary policies that created more problems than they solved.

Financial news outlets, such as The Wall Street Journal, Bloomberg, and CNBC, focused on the stock market volatility and business reactions to tariffs. They provided in-depth analysis on how tariffs disrupted supply chains, increased costs for corporations, and slowed business investment due to economic uncertainty. Reports frequently highlighted concerns from business leaders and economists who warned that tariffs could lead to inflation and reduced global trade competitiveness for American firms. At the same time, some financial analysts acknowledged that tariffs did put pressure on China, forcing the country to reassess its trade practices and consider structural economic changes. This more pragmatic, data-driven coverage differed from the politically charged narratives seen in mainstream media.

As the trade war unfolded, public perception of tariffs was deeply influenced by which media sources people trusted and consumed. Trump supporters who followed conservative media were more likely to view tariffs as a necessary fight for economic independence, while those consuming liberal-leaning news saw tariffs as harmful, inflationary policies. Independent voters and business leaders often turned to financial news for a more neutral, analytical perspective, weighing the risks and benefits of tariffs on long-term economic growth. In the end, media narratives helped shape the broader debate, reinforcing partisan divides while also influencing how everyday Americans understood the real-world effects of Trump's trade policies.

Chapter 9
The Global Ripple Effect of the U.S.-China Trade War

The U.S.-China trade war, initiated under the Trump administration, had far-reaching consequences that extended beyond the two economic superpowers. While the trade dispute was framed as an effort to correct unfair trade practices, reduce the U.S. trade deficit, and protect American industries, its impact was felt across the global economy. As tariffs escalated and retaliatory measures were imposed, international markets experienced supply chain disruptions, shifts in trade alliances, and economic uncertainty. Many countries found themselves caught in the crossfire, either benefiting from the trade war as businesses sought alternative supply chains or suffering losses due to decreased global demand and economic instability.

Asian economies were among the most significantly affected, particularly nations that had strong trade relationships with both the U.S. and China. Countries such as Vietnam, India, Taiwan, and South Korea saw increased investment as companies diversified their supply chains to avoid tariffs, making them unexpected winners of the trade conflict. However, other economies, including those in Southeast Asia and Latin America, struggled as global trade flows slowed, leading to weaker economic growth and uncertainty in export-driven industries. Meanwhile, Europe found itself facing a complex trade environment, as the European Union had to navigate deteriorating relations with both the U.S. and China, while simultaneously attempting to strengthen its own trade policies to mitigate the fallout.

Beyond economic shifts, the trade war reshaped global diplomatic relations, influencing how nations approached trade policy, economic alliances, and strategic partnerships. Countries that had traditionally relied on the U.S. and China for trade were forced to reevaluate their long-term economic strategies, balancing between the two superpowers. The trade war also intensified technological competition, particularly in sectors such as 5G, artificial intelligence, and semiconductor production, with governments worldwide seeking to reduce dependency on foreign technology. As the global economy adjusted to these new realities, it became clear that the effects of the U.S.-China trade war extended well beyond tariffs, influencing long-term international trade policies and economic stability in ways that would last for years to come.

Asian Economies: Winners and Losers

The U.S.-China trade war had a profound impact on Asian economies, creating both winners and losers as global trade patterns shifted. While some countries benefited from supply chain diversification, others suffered from export declines, increased costs, and economic instability. As U.S. tariffs on Chinese goods increased, businesses sought alternative manufacturing hubs to avoid higher costs, leading to a boom in certain Asian economies. However, countries heavily dependent on trade with China faced economic setbacks, as China's slowing economy and retaliatory tariffs disrupted regional markets. The trade war reshaped Asia's economic landscape, forcing nations to adapt, innovate, or struggle with uncertainty.

Among the biggest winners of the trade war were Vietnam, India, Taiwan, and Malaysia, as they became attractive alternatives for companies shifting production away from China. Vietnam, in particular, emerged as a key beneficiary, with major companies like Samsung, Apple, and Nike expanding manufacturing operations there to circumvent U.S. tariffs on Chinese exports. The country saw a surge in foreign direct investment (FDI) as businesses moved electronics, textiles, and consumer goods production to Vietnamese factories. Similarly, India positioned itself as a manufacturing hub, especially in sectors like smartphones, automobiles, and pharmaceuticals. Companies like Apple and Foxconn increased investments in Indian production facilities, aligning with India's "Make in India" initiative, which sought to reduce reliance on Chinese imports. Taiwan also gained, as its semiconductor industry — home to TSMC, the world's leading chipmaker — became crucial in the U.S.-China tech competition, receiving increased orders from American firms seeking to reduce dependency on Chinese supply chains.

Despite these gains, several Asian economies found themselves negatively impacted by the trade war, particularly those closely linked to China's economic growth. Countries such as South Korea, Japan, and Thailand saw reduced demand for exports, as China's economic slowdown affected regional trade and supply chains. South Korea, for example, struggled with declining semiconductor exports, as major Chinese buyers reduced orders due to weaker demand and supply chain disruptions. Similarly, Japan, which had strong trade ties with both the U.S. and China, faced diplomatic and economic uncertainty, particularly in the automobile and electronics industries. Thailand's economy also suffered, as Chinese tourists — one of its main sources of revenue—declined due to economic uncertainty and reduced consumer spending.

Another loser of the trade war was China itself, as its economy experienced slower growth, declining exports, and rising production costs. While China retaliated with its own tariffs on American goods, these measures did little to counteract the damage done by U.S. trade restrictions. Chinese manufacturers faced higher costs and supply chain disruptions, forcing some to move production abroad to avoid tariffs. Additionally, the technology sector suffered, as U.S. restrictions on Chinese tech companies—such as Huawei and ZTE—limited their access to critical American components.

Overall, the trade war redistributed economic opportunities across Asia, creating winners among countries that could attract new investment while hurting those that remained tied to China's economic fortunes. As trade tensions continued, Asian economies had to adapt their strategies, focusing on strengthening regional trade agreements, diversifying markets, and investing in new industries to remain competitive in the shifting global landscape.

European Markets and Their Response to U.S. Protectionism

The U.S.-China trade war and the Trump administration's broader protectionist policies significantly affected European markets, forcing the European Union (EU) and individual nations to reevaluate their trade strategies, economic policies, and diplomatic relationships. While Trump's tariffs primarily targeted China, his administration also imposed tariffs on European steel, aluminum, and other goods, escalating trade tensions between the U.S. and its traditional allies. The EU, known for its strong stance on free trade, found itself in a challenging position—balancing economic ties with both the U.S. and China while trying to protect European industries from rising trade barriers. The response from European markets included retaliatory tariffs, stronger regional trade agreements, and efforts to reduce dependence on U.S. and Chinese markets.

One of the most direct impacts of U.S. protectionism on Europe was the imposition of tariffs on European steel and aluminum in 2018, under Section 232 of the Trade Expansion Act. The Trump administration justified these tariffs on national security grounds, arguing that foreign steel imports threatened the viability of U.S. domestic production. This move infuriated EU leaders, who saw it as an unjustified attack on transatlantic trade. In response, the EU imposed retaliatory tariffs on American goods, targeting industries in politically sensitive states. Products like Harley-Davidson motorcycles, bourbon whiskey, and Levi's jeans were hit with additional tariffs, directly affecting American manufacturers. The EU also filed a complaint with the World Trade Organization (WTO), arguing that the U.S. steel and aluminum tariffs violated international trade laws.

Beyond retaliatory measures, Europe sought to diversify its trade relationships to reduce dependence on the U.S. and China. The EU strengthened its economic partnerships with Asian and Latin American countries, signing trade agreements with Japan, Canada, and the Mercosur bloc (Argentina, Brazil, Paraguay, and Uruguay). The EU-Japan Economic Partnership Agreement (EPA), which came into effect in 2019, created the world's largest open trade zone, eliminating tariffs on nearly all goods traded between the two economies. This agreement was seen as a direct response to U.S. protectionism, reinforcing the EU's commitment to free trade and multilateralism. Additionally, the EU deepened its economic ties with China, despite concerns over human rights and trade imbalances. In

December 2020, the EU and China finalized the Comprehensive Agreement on Investment (CAI), aiming to provide European businesses with better access to Chinese markets.

However, Europe's closer ties with China also raised concerns about economic dependency and geopolitical risks. While some EU nations, particularly Germany and France, saw economic opportunities in stronger trade relations with China, others warned about the risks of Chinese influence over critical industries. The Trump administration pressured European allies to limit cooperation with Chinese technology firms, particularly in the development of 5G networks. The U.S. lobbied EU nations to ban Huawei from their telecommunications infrastructure, citing security risks. Some European governments, including the UK and Sweden, ultimately restricted or banned Huawei's 5G equipment, aligning with the U.S. position.

As the Biden administration took office, the EU signaled its willingness to rebuild transatlantic trade relations, but many European nations remained wary of future U.S. protectionist measures. The trade tensions under Trump's presidency pushed Europe to become more self-reliant, strengthen its regional trade networks, and reduce its vulnerability to external trade disruptions. Moving forward, European markets will likely continue balancing economic cooperation with the U.S. while pursuing more independent trade policies to safeguard their economic interests.

Developing Nations and Supply Chain Disruptions

The U.S.-China trade war and its impact on global supply chains significantly affected developing nations, many of which rely heavily on trade, foreign investment, and stable global markets. As tariffs escalated and multinational corporations looked for alternatives to avoid higher costs, some developing countries saw an opportunity to expand their manufacturing sectors, while others faced economic setbacks due to declining exports, disrupted supply routes, and shifting trade relationships. The resulting instability forced many developing nations to reassess their economic strategies, infrastructure capabilities, and long-term trade policies to remain competitive in the evolving global marketplace.

For some nations, the trade war created a surge in economic opportunities as companies sought to relocate manufacturing operations outside of China. Vietnam, India, Indonesia, and Bangladesh became prime destinations for industries looking to establish new production hubs. Vietnam, in particular, benefited from the relocation of electronics and textile manufacturing, with major corporations like Samsung, Apple, and Nike expanding operations in the country. India also positioned itself as a key player in global smartphone manufacturing, attracting investments from companies like Foxconn and Wistron. This shift allowed these countries to create jobs, boost exports, and attract foreign investment, strengthening their role in global supply chains. However, the rapid influx of manufacturing posed significant challenges, as many of these nations lacked the necessary infrastructure, regulatory efficiency, and skilled labor to accommodate such a sudden shift. In some cases, logistical bottlenecks, bureaucratic delays, and rising labor costs made it difficult for companies to fully transition operations, highlighting the complexities of supply chain realignment.

On the other hand, many developing nations that had close economic ties to China and the United States experienced negative consequences as global trade slowed. Several economies, particularly those in Africa, Latin America, and Southeast Asia, depend on China as a primary trading partner, exporting raw materials, agricultural products, and intermediate goods to fuel Chinese manufacturing. As U.S. tariffs led to a slowdown in Chinese exports, demand for these raw materials decreased, causing economic downturns in countries like Brazil, South Africa, and Indonesia. This decline in demand for commodities resulted in reduced revenues, job losses, and increased financial strain on governments that rely on trade for economic stability. Additionally, many small and medium-sized enterprises in developing nations suffered from rising production costs, as they depended on Chinese-made components to assemble goods for export. The increased cost of imported materials, combined with delays in shipping and fluctuating exchange rates, created financial challenges for businesses that struggled to adapt to the changing landscape.

The trade war also discouraged foreign direct investment in some developing economies, as multinational corporations became more cautious about expanding into markets affected by trade instability. This lack of investment hindered industrial growth and job creation in countries that had previously benefited from globalization. In response to these disruptions, many developing nations sought to strengthen regional trade agreements, improve industrial capacity, and diversify their economies to reduce reliance on any single global power. Regional organizations such as ASEAN and the African Continental Free Trade Area (AfCFTA) worked to enhance intra-regional trade to mitigate dependence on external supply chains. Some governments also increased investments in digital infrastructure and automation to modernize their manufacturing sectors and remain competitive.

The long-term effects of the trade war on developing nations underscored the vulnerabilities of global supply chains and the need for economic resilience. While some countries were able to capitalize on shifting trade dynamics and attract new investments, others struggled with economic downturns, lost exports, and financial instability. Moving forward, developing economies must focus on building sustainable and flexible trade policies, investing in local industries, and strengthening regional partnerships to ensure long-term stability in an unpredictable global economic environment.

The Role of International Trade Organizations

The role of international trade organizations became increasingly critical during the U.S.-China trade war, as these institutions were tasked with managing disputes, ensuring fair trade practices, and mitigating the broader economic fallout of escalating tariffs. Organizations such as the World Trade Organization (WTO), International Monetary Fund (IMF), World Bank, and regional trade alliances played key roles in addressing the disruptions caused by protectionist policies, retaliatory tariffs, and shifting global supply chains. While these organizations were established to promote stability, transparency, and economic cooperation, their effectiveness in handling the trade war was debated, with some arguing that their influence was limited in curbing unilateral actions by major economies.

The World Trade Organization (WTO) was at the center of the conflict, as both the U.S. and China were bound by its trade regulations. The WTO was created to provide a structured mechanism for resolving disputes, ensuring that countries adhere to agreed-upon trade rules. However, during the trade war, the Trump administration bypassed traditional WTO dispute mechanisms, arguing that the organization had failed to adequately address China's unfair trade practices, including intellectual property theft, forced technology transfers, and state subsidies to Chinese firms. The

U.S. imposed tariffs without seeking WTO approval, claiming national security concerns and economic necessity as justification. China, in turn, filed multiple complaints against the U.S. at the WTO, arguing that the tariffs violated global trade rules. While the WTO acknowledged that some of the U.S. tariffs were inconsistent with its regulations, it lacked enforcement power, leading to further skepticism about its ability to effectively mediate trade disputes between superpowers.

The International Monetary Fund (IMF) and the World Bank played important but indirect roles in addressing the economic consequences of the trade war. The IMF repeatedly warned of the global risks associated with rising protectionism, estimating that the trade war would reduce global GDP growth due to reduced trade volumes, increased business uncertainty, and disrupted investment flows. Developing economies, which relied on stable trade environments to attract foreign direct investment, were particularly vulnerable. The IMF encouraged both the U.S. and China to negotiate a resolution, emphasizing that prolonged trade disputes could trigger economic slowdowns and financial instability in emerging markets. Meanwhile, the World Bank worked to support nations affected by trade disruptions, particularly countries reliant on commodity exports to China. The institution provided policy recommendations, economic forecasting, and financial assistance to mitigate the economic impact of falling trade revenues.

Regional trade organizations also played a role in reshaping global trade dynamics during the conflict. The European Union (EU), Association of Southeast Asian Nations (ASEAN), and African Continental Free Trade Area (AfCFTA) sought to strengthen intra-regional trade agreements to reduce reliance on both the U.S. and China. The EU pursued trade deals with Japan, Canada, and

Mercosur, while ASEAN nations worked to attract companies looking to relocate manufacturing operations away from China. The Regional Comprehensive Economic Partnership (RCEP), a trade agreement including China, Japan, South Korea, Australia, and ASEAN countries, was seen as a strategic move to counterbalance U.S. trade policies and solidify Asian economic cooperation.

The effectiveness of international trade organizations in managing the trade war remains a subject of debate. While these institutions played a crucial role in monitoring economic impacts, issuing policy guidance, and facilitating diplomatic engagement, they struggled to enforce trade rules or prevent economic disruptions caused by unilateral actions. The trade war exposed the limitations of global trade governance, raising questions about how these organizations can be reformed to better address future trade conflicts in an increasingly multipolar world economy. Moving forward, these institutions will need to adapt to new geopolitical realities, enhance their enforcement mechanisms, and foster greater economic cooperation to ensure that global trade remains stable, fair, and mutually beneficial for all nations.

Chapter 10
The Future of U.S. Manufacturing in a Post-Tariff Economy

The future of U.S. manufacturing in a post-tariff economy is shaped by the lessons learned from the trade war, the restructuring of global supply chains, and the need for technological advancement to maintain competitiveness. The tariffs imposed during the Trump administration were intended to revitalize domestic production, encourage companies to reshore jobs, and reduce reliance on foreign imports, particularly from China. While some industries saw short-term gains, the long-term effects were more complex, with increased costs, retaliatory tariffs, and supply chain disruptions creating challenges for many businesses. As the U.S. moves beyond the trade war, manufacturing must adapt to new economic realities, balancing economic nationalism with global market demands.

One of the key trends in post-tariff U.S. manufacturing is the shift toward automation, advanced technology, and regional supply chain diversification. While tariffs aimed to protect American workers, many companies found that rising production costs made it more efficient to invest in robotics, artificial intelligence, and smart manufacturing rather than expand their domestic workforce. Additionally, instead of bringing all production back to the U.S., many firms have opted to relocate operations to other low-cost countries like Vietnam, Mexico, and India, diversifying their supply chains while avoiding dependence on China. This shift suggests that rather than a full resurgence of traditional manufacturing jobs, the industry is evolving toward a more technologically driven and regionally balanced model.

Government policy will play a crucial role in shaping the future of U.S. manufacturing, determining whether the country can truly reduce dependency on foreign production while maintaining competitiveness in a global economy. The Biden administration's focus on domestic investment through initiatives like the CHIPS Act, clean energy incentives, and infrastructure spending suggests a different approach to industrial growth—one that prioritizes incentives over protectionist tariffs. However, manufacturing success will ultimately depend on how businesses adapt to changing consumer demands, labor market challenges, and geopolitical uncertainties. As the U.S. manufacturing sector moves forward, it must embrace innovation, workforce development, and strategic partnerships to ensure that the industry remains strong, resilient, and competitive in the post-tariff era.

Reshoring and Automation: The New Industrial Revolution?

The future of U.S. manufacturing is being reshaped by reshoring and automation, two forces driving what many are calling a new industrial revolution. The push to bring manufacturing back to the United States intensified during the U.S.-China trade war, as tariffs exposed the vulnerabilities of global supply chains and highlighted the risks of overdependence on foreign production, particularly from China. While tariffs were initially designed to encourage reshoring, their impact was mixed, as many companies instead sought alternative low-cost manufacturing hubs in countries like Vietnam, India, and Mexico. However, recent developments—including geopolitical tensions, supply chain disruptions from the COVID-19 pandemic, and advances in manufacturing technology—have renewed the focus on making domestic production more viable through automation and smart manufacturing.

Reshoring has become a key priority for U.S. policymakers and businesses alike, as companies seek to reduce reliance on foreign suppliers and improve supply chain resilience. Industries such as semiconductors, pharmaceuticals, and clean energy technologies have received significant government support to encourage domestic production. The CHIPS and Science Act, passed in 2022, is a prime example of the federal government's commitment to boosting domestic semiconductor manufacturing, reducing the U.S.'s dependence on Taiwan and China for advanced microchips. Similarly, incentives for electric vehicle (EV) battery production and renewable energy technology aim to ensure that the U.S. is not left behind in critical industries of the future. However, despite these initiatives, reshoring remains challenging, as high labor costs, regulatory complexities, and a shortage of skilled workers make large-scale domestic production difficult.

This is where automation and advanced manufacturing technologies come into play. Companies looking to reshore operations are investing heavily in robotics, artificial intelligence (AI), and smart factories to offset the higher costs of U.S. production. Automation allows manufacturers to increase efficiency, reduce dependency on human labor, and maintain global competitiveness. For example, industries such as automobile manufacturing, electronics, and logistics have increasingly integrated machine learning and robotic assembly lines to enhance productivity while reducing labor costs. Amazon, for instance, has adopted automated fulfillment centers, while Tesla continues to refine robot-assisted production in its U.S.-based factories. These technological advancements suggest that the future of reshored manufacturing may look very different from the traditional factory model, with fewer but higher-skilled jobs required to operate and maintain automated production systems.

While automation offers many advantages, it also raises concerns about job displacement. Historically, manufacturing jobs provided stable, well-paying employment for millions of American workers, but as machines take on more production tasks, there is growing anxiety about the loss of traditional blue-collar jobs. Some argue that instead of completely eliminating jobs, automation will transform the labor market, shifting demand toward highly skilled technicians, engineers, and programmers who can develop, manage, and repair automated systems. To address this, many policymakers and industry leaders are advocating for workforce retraining programs and investments in STEM education, ensuring that American workers can adapt to the changing industrial landscape.

The reshoring movement and the rise of automation represent a new chapter for U.S. manufacturing, one that balances economic security with technological progress. While reshoring efforts may not fully restore traditional factory jobs, they will create new opportunities in advanced manufacturing, AI-driven production, and supply chain innovation. The success of this new industrial revolution will depend on how well the U.S. navigates workforce development, infrastructure investment, and international trade relations, ensuring that manufacturing remains a core pillar of American economic strength in the decades to come.

Labor Market Challenges: Job Creation vs. Job Displacement

The transformation of U.S. manufacturing in a post-tariff economy presents a paradox: while reshoring efforts and automation have the potential to create new jobs, they also pose a significant risk of job displacement. The tension between revitalizing domestic industry and the growing reliance on technology is reshaping the American labor market, requiring both workers and policymakers to adapt. The push to bring manufacturing back to the U.S. was driven by tariffs, supply chain disruptions, and geopolitical concerns, but the reality of higher labor costs and the efficiency of automation has complicated the promise of widespread job creation. Instead of a return to traditional manufacturing employment, the sector is undergoing a shift toward high-tech production, demanding new skills and workforce adaptations.

One of the major challenges in job creation is finding a balance between reshoring efforts and the need for a skilled workforce. As companies relocate production facilities to the U.S., they often struggle to find workers with the necessary technical skills to operate advanced manufacturing systems, robotics, and AI-driven production lines. The rise of smart factories means that traditional assembly line jobs are being replaced by positions that require expertise in computer programming, engineering, and machine maintenance. This shift has created a gap between job availability and workforce readiness, leaving many positions unfilled. Companies are calling for more investment in STEM education, vocational training, and apprenticeships to help workers transition into the new era of manufacturing. However, without significant retraining initiatives, many blue-collar workers who lost jobs due to outsourcing may struggle to find employment in the reshaped labor market.

At the same time, automation poses a major threat to job security, particularly in industries where robotics can increase efficiency and reduce costs. Companies looking to remain competitive in a global market are investing in automation to minimize reliance on human labor, reducing the number of jobs available in traditional manufacturing roles. The automotive and logistics industries are prime examples of this trend, with automated assembly lines and AI-powered warehouses becoming more common. While automation increases productivity and profitability, it also leads to job displacement, particularly for workers without specialized technical training. The risk is that reshoring efforts may not result in a proportional increase in employment, as companies choose to automate rather than hire large numbers of workers.

Despite these challenges, there are opportunities for job creation in new sectors, particularly in advanced manufacturing, clean energy, and technology-driven industries. The demand for highly skilled workers in semiconductor manufacturing, renewable energy production, and AI-driven logistics is growing, and government incentives, such as the CHIPS Act and infrastructure investments, aim to support workforce development. The key to ensuring that reshoring benefits American workers will be expanding access to retraining programs, encouraging public-private partnerships in workforce education, and incentivizing businesses to invest in human capital alongside automation.

The future of U.S. manufacturing and the labor market will be shaped by how effectively the country adapts to technological advancements and economic shifts. While automation will inevitably replace some jobs, strategic investments in education, skills development, and workforce retraining can ensure that American workers are not left behind. The challenge ahead is to strike a balance between economic growth and job security, making sure that the benefits of reshoring and technological progress extend to workers across all levels of the economy.

The Role of Government Incentives

The role of government incentives in shaping the future of U.S. manufacturing has become increasingly important in a post-tariff economy, as policymakers seek to balance economic security, job creation, and global competitiveness. While tariffs were initially introduced as a way to protect domestic industries and encourage reshoring, their long-term effectiveness was limited due to higher production costs, supply chain disruptions, and retaliatory trade measures. As a result, the U.S. government has shifted toward targeted incentives, investment programs, and tax benefits to encourage companies to manufacture domestically without relying on broad trade restrictions. These incentives aim to spur innovation, strengthen supply chain resilience, and create high-paying jobs, ensuring that the U.S. remains a leader in advanced manufacturing.

One of the most significant examples of government-driven industrial policy is the CHIPS and Science Act, which was passed to boost domestic semiconductor manufacturing. The semiconductor industry is critical to modern technology, powering everything from smartphones and automobiles to medical devices and defense systems. Over the years, offshoring led to heavy reliance on Taiwan, South Korea, and China for semiconductor production, creating major vulnerabilities for the U.S. economy. The CHIPS Act provides billions of dollars in subsidies, research funding, and tax incentives to encourage companies like Intel, TSMC, and Samsung to build semiconductor fabrication plants in the U.S. This policy aims to strengthen national security, reduce dependence on foreign suppliers, and create thousands of high-tech jobs in regions that historically relied on manufacturing.

Beyond semiconductors, the clean energy and electric vehicle (EV) industries have also become key areas of government-supported manufacturing growth. The Inflation Reduction Act (IRA), passed in 2022, includes tax credits, grants, and subsidies to accelerate domestic production of solar panels, wind turbines, EV batteries, and other green technologies. The goal is to reduce reliance on Chinese-made clean energy components while simultaneously addressing climate change and positioning the U.S. as a global leader in renewable energy manufacturing. Companies that establish EV battery plants and solar panel factories within the U.S. benefit from significant financial incentives, helping to create jobs in areas affected by industrial decline.

The federal government has also introduced workforce development incentives to address labor shortages and skill gaps in the manufacturing sector. Programs offering tax credits for employee training, partnerships between community colleges and industrial employers, and grants for workforce retraining aim to ensure that American workers can fill the high-tech jobs created by reshoring efforts. These initiatives recognize that bringing manufacturing back to the U.S. requires not just factories, but also a skilled workforce capable of operating advanced machinery and AI-driven production systems.

While government incentives play a crucial role in supporting manufacturing, they also raise long-term questions about sustainability and effectiveness. Some critics argue that subsidies and tax breaks may lead to short-term economic gains but fail to create lasting industrial growth if companies later relocate for lower labor costs elsewhere. Others question whether these incentives disproportionately benefit large corporations while small and mid-sized manufacturers struggle to compete.

Despite these concerns, government incentives remain a key tool for ensuring that U.S. manufacturing remains competitive in a rapidly changing global economy. By strategically targeting industries vital to national security, technological advancement, and clean energy, these policies can stimulate innovation, create high-paying jobs, and build a more resilient industrial base, positioning the U.S. for long-term success in global trade and production.

Building a Competitive Domestic Industry Without Tariffs

Building a competitive domestic industry without tariffs requires a strategic combination of investment, innovation, workforce development, and smart trade policies. While tariffs were introduced as a way to protect American industries from foreign competition, their long-term effectiveness was limited due to rising costs for businesses, retaliatory trade measures, and disruptions in global supply chains. Instead of relying on protectionist policies that can isolate the U.S. from global trade opportunities, a more sustainable approach involves government incentives, infrastructure improvements, technological advancements, and investment in workforce training to ensure that American industries can compete globally without artificial trade barriers.

One of the most effective ways to strengthen domestic industry is through targeted government investment in key sectors such as advanced manufacturing, semiconductors, clean energy, and biotechnology. The CHIPS and Science Act, for example, provides billions of dollars in subsidies and tax incentives to encourage companies to build semiconductor manufacturing plants in the U.S., reducing reliance on foreign suppliers. Similarly, the Inflation Reduction Act (IRA) supports domestic clean energy production, helping the U.S. become a leader in electric vehicle (EV) batteries, wind turbines, and solar panels. These investments ensure that American companies can compete in high-tech industries, where labor costs are less of a factor and innovation drives success.

Another critical factor in building a competitive domestic industry is strengthening supply chains and infrastructure. The COVID-19 pandemic and the U.S.-China trade war exposed major vulnerabilities in global supply networks, with shortages of medical supplies, semiconductors, and raw materials highlighting the risks of overreliance on foreign production. To address this, reshoring efforts should focus on rebuilding critical supply chains within North America, including through partnerships with Mexico and Canada under the USMCA (United States-Mexico-Canada Agreement). Investing in modern transportation, energy, and broadband infrastructure is also essential for making U.S. manufacturing more efficient and cost-effective, reducing logistical hurdles that have made offshore production more attractive in the past.

Innovation and automation play a key role in ensuring competitiveness without tariffs. Rather than trying to compete with low-wage countries on labor costs, U.S. industries should focus on leveraging technology, robotics, and AI-driven production systems to enhance productivity. Automation reduces dependence on cheap labor, allowing companies to maintain high production output while keeping costs manageable. The rise of smart factories and 3D printing also provides opportunities for on-demand production, reducing reliance on overseas suppliers and enabling companies to adapt quickly to market changes. By embracing cutting-edge manufacturing techniques, the U.S. can maintain a strong industrial base without resorting to trade restrictions.

Developing a highly skilled workforce is another essential component of a strong domestic industry. Many American companies struggle to find workers with the technical expertise needed to operate advanced manufacturing systems, highlighting the need for investment in vocational training, STEM education, and apprenticeships. Public-private partnerships between universities, technical schools, and manufacturers can ensure that the next generation of workers is prepared for high-tech, high-paying jobs, reducing the need to outsource labor.

Finally, smart trade policies and diplomatic engagement can help build a thriving domestic industry without relying on tariffs. The U.S. should focus on negotiating fair trade agreements, enforcing intellectual property protections, and securing access to critical raw materials through strategic alliances. Rather than isolating itself, the U.S. can collaborate with allies to establish trade rules that benefit domestic industries while maintaining access to global markets.

By focusing on innovation, supply chain resilience, workforce development, and strategic trade policies, the U.S. can strengthen its industrial base without the economic risks of protectionist tariffs. This approach ensures long-term growth, global competitiveness, and economic security, making American industries more resilient, adaptive, and successful in the evolving world economy.

Chapter 11
Economic Recovery and the Lessons for Future Trade Policy

The aftermath of the U.S.-China trade war and the broader use of tariffs under the Trump administration have provided valuable insights into the complex relationship between trade policy, economic growth, and global market stability. While tariffs were implemented as a tool to revitalize American manufacturing, reduce trade deficits, and protect domestic industries, their long-term effects revealed both intended and unintended consequences. Some industries saw short-term benefits, but many businesses and consumers experienced higher costs, supply chain disruptions, and economic uncertainty. As the U.S. moves forward, economic recovery depends on learning from these past trade policies and crafting a more balanced, strategic approach that ensures domestic competitiveness while maintaining strong international partnerships.

One of the key lessons from the trade war is that tariffs alone are not a sustainable solution for economic growth. While they can provide temporary relief for certain industries, they also increase production costs, reduce global competitiveness, and trigger retaliatory measures from other nations. The economic fallout from the trade war highlighted the importance of diversifying supply chains, strengthening domestic industrial capabilities, and investing in long-term economic resilience rather than relying on protectionist measures. Future trade policy must strike a balance between economic nationalism and global trade engagement, ensuring that U.S. industries can compete fairly without being isolated from global markets.

As the U.S. continues its economic recovery, policymakers must take a holistic approach to trade policy, focusing on strategic investments in innovation, infrastructure, and workforce development. Trade agreements should be structured to promote fair competition while fostering collaboration with allies, allowing for greater economic stability. Additionally, the role of automation, clean energy, and emerging technologies will play a crucial role in shaping the next phase of industrial growth. By applying the lessons learned from the tariff wars, the U.S. can create a trade policy that ensures long-term economic prosperity, minimizes disruptions, and supports a competitive yet sustainable domestic industry.

Key Takeaways for Future Administrations

The U.S.-China trade war and the broader use of tariffs under the Trump administration provided critical lessons for future administrations, shaping how trade policy should be approached to ensure economic stability, industrial competitiveness, and diplomatic strength. While tariffs were initially used as a strategic tool to counter unfair trade practices, reduce trade deficits, and protect American industries, their long-term effects demonstrated both the benefits and limitations of aggressive protectionist measures. Future administrations must take a more balanced, strategic approach to trade policy—one that leverages diplomatic engagement, technological advancements, and targeted economic incentives rather than relying solely on tariffs.

One of the most important takeaways is that tariffs alone cannot revive domestic manufacturing or ensure economic security. While they provided short-term relief for certain industries such as steel and aluminum, they also increased production costs for businesses that relied on imported raw materials, leading to higher prices for consumers. Many companies passed these costs onto customers or sought alternative suppliers outside of China, demonstrating that tariffs often shift supply chains rather than bringing jobs back to the U.S. Future administrations should focus on investment in domestic production capabilities rather than using tariffs as a long-term solution.

Another key lesson is that retaliatory tariffs can create unintended economic consequences, particularly for industries that rely on global trade and exports. When China responded to U.S. tariffs by placing its own restrictions on American goods, sectors like agriculture, technology, and manufacturing suffered severe setbacks. American farmers, who depend on China as a key export market for soybeans, pork, and other agricultural products, were among the hardest hit. Future administrations must recognize that trade wars rarely lead to outright victories and should work toward negotiated trade agreements that avoid prolonged economic disruptions.

A major takeaway from the trade war is the importance of supply chain resilience and diversification. The tariffs, combined with the COVID-19 pandemic, exposed how vulnerable American industries had become to foreign supply chains, particularly in sectors like semiconductors, pharmaceuticals, and critical minerals. Future administrations must prioritize reshoring key industries while also fostering regional trade partnerships to create more flexible, secure supply chains. Strengthening relationships with Mexico, Canada, and other strategic partners under agreements like the USMCA can help reduce reliance on countries like China while maintaining the benefits of globalization.

Additionally, future administrations should emphasize technological investment and workforce development as central pillars of trade policy. As manufacturing becomes more reliant on automation, AI, and robotics, the U.S. must train workers for the jobs of the future rather than attempting to restore outdated manufacturing models. Investing in STEM education, vocational training, and apprenticeship programs will ensure that American workers are equipped for high-tech, high-wage industries, making the U.S. more competitive without needing trade restrictions to protect outdated jobs.

Ultimately, the trade war showed that a well-rounded trade strategy must incorporate diplomacy, domestic investment, and global cooperation rather than relying on unilateral economic measures. Future administrations should balance economic security with global trade engagement, ensuring that U.S. industries can compete in emerging markets while safeguarding critical sectors. By applying these lessons, the U.S. can strengthen its industrial base, maintain leadership in innovation, and build a more resilient, adaptive economy in an increasingly complex global trade environment.

Trade Policy in a Changing Global Order

Trade policy in a changing global order is becoming increasingly complex, shaped by shifting geopolitical alliances, technological advancements, and economic disruptions. The traditional models of global trade, where multilateral agreements and free markets dominated, are being challenged by economic nationalism, supply chain vulnerabilities, and growing tensions between major economies like the U.S. and China. As the world moves away from an era of unregulated globalization, nations are rethinking their trade strategies to balance economic security with international cooperation. The future of trade policy will depend on how well countries adapt to new economic realities, technological shifts, and evolving geopolitical landscapes while maintaining global stability.

One of the most significant trends in global trade policy is the rise of economic nationalism and strategic trade partnerships. Countries are moving away from purely free-market principles and prioritizing domestic economic security, job protection, and industry resilience. The U.S., under both the Trump and Biden administrations, has focused on reshoring critical industries, reducing reliance on China, and promoting regional trade partnerships such as the United States-Mexico-Canada Agreement (USMCA). Similarly, the European Union has introduced policies to strengthen supply chains within the region and ensure that key industries remain competitive in a rapidly changing global economy. While economic nationalism can protect domestic jobs and industries, it also risks trade fragmentation, higher costs for consumers, and reduced global economic cooperation.

Another major factor shaping trade policy is the increasing importance of supply chain resilience and diversification. The COVID-19 pandemic, combined with the U.S.-China trade war, revealed how fragile global supply chains had become, particularly in key sectors such as semiconductors, pharmaceuticals, and clean energy technologies. Many countries are now working to reduce dependency on a single foreign supplier, leading to the rise of nearshoring and friend-shoring strategies—where companies relocate production to allied nations with stable trade agreements. For example, the U.S. is working with Mexico, Canada, India, and Vietnam to develop alternative supply networks, ensuring that critical industries are less vulnerable to geopolitical disruptions. This shift reflects a broader movement toward regional trade agreements and economic blocs, where countries collaborate with trusted partners to reduce risk and increase economic security.

Technology is also playing a transformative role in global trade policy, particularly with the rise of automation, artificial intelligence, and digital trade agreements. As manufacturing becomes more automated, the traditional advantage of low-cost labor markets is diminishing, allowing advanced economies like the U.S. and Europe to reclaim industrial production without depending on offshore labor. Meanwhile, digital trade agreements are redefining commerce, as countries focus on protecting intellectual property, regulating e-commerce, and securing data flows across borders. Nations that invest in technology, digital infrastructure, and workforce training will have a significant advantage in the global economy, as trade shifts from physical goods to digital services and advanced manufacturing.

As global trade policies evolve, balancing economic security with international cooperation will be crucial. Countries must find ways to protect domestic industries while maintaining strong international relationships, ensuring that trade remains a driver of economic growth rather than a source of geopolitical conflict. Future trade agreements will likely focus on regional partnerships, technological collaboration, and sustainable trade practices, reflecting the new realities of a shifting global economy. By embracing innovation and strategic diplomacy, nations can navigate the complexities of modern trade while securing long-term economic stability and global competitiveness.

Balancing Protectionism with Globalization

Balancing protectionism with globalization has become one of the most critical challenges in modern trade policy. While globalization has historically driven economic growth, increased market access, and technological advancements, it has also led to outsourcing, industrial decline in developed economies, and supply chain vulnerabilities. In response, many nations have turned to protectionist policies, such as tariffs, subsidies, and domestic production mandates, to safeguard key industries and jobs. However, an overly protectionist approach risks isolating economies, raising costs for consumers, and reducing trade partnerships. The challenge for policymakers is to strike a balance between economic security and international cooperation, ensuring that domestic industries thrive without cutting off the benefits of global trade.

One of the main reasons for increased protectionism is the desire to strengthen national industries and reduce dependency on foreign manufacturing. The U.S.-China trade war highlighted the risks of over-reliance on global supply chains, particularly in critical sectors like semiconductors, pharmaceuticals, and energy production. In response, the U.S. and other nations have implemented policies aimed at reshoring key industries, such as the CHIPS and Science Act, which provides financial incentives for domestic semiconductor manufacturing. Similarly, the Inflation Reduction Act (IRA) promotes U.S.-based production of clean energy technologies, ensuring that industries crucial for future economic security remain under national control. While these policies help protect domestic industries, they also create tensions with global trade partners, as foreign companies and governments see these measures as forms of economic favoritism that violate free trade principles.

At the same time, complete economic isolation is not a viable option in an interconnected world. Globalization has enabled businesses to access larger markets, cheaper raw materials, and diversified supply chains, making production more efficient and cost-effective. Even as countries implement protectionist policies, they must continue engaging in global trade agreements, securing access to key markets, and investing in strategic partnerships. For example, the U.S. has strengthened ties with Mexico and Canada through the USMCA, ensuring that trade flows remain robust within North America. The European Union continues to negotiate trade deals with Japan, Australia, and developing economies, seeking to build resilient trade relationships that balance domestic economic interests with global connectivity.

A smart trade policy must focus on building domestic industrial strength while maintaining global trade cooperation. This can be achieved through targeted government incentives, investment in innovation, and workforce development rather than broad tariffs that disrupt supply chains. Investing in automation, artificial intelligence, and digital trade will allow economies to compete on technology and productivity rather than low labor costs, reducing the need for protectionist barriers. Moreover, modern trade agreements should emphasize fair competition, sustainable production, and technological collaboration, ensuring that economic growth is mutually beneficial rather than exploitative.

In the long run, balancing protectionism with globalization requires a strategic, adaptable trade policy that protects national interests while embracing the benefits of international economic integration. By focusing on industrial modernization, fair trade enforcement, and regional trade alliances, nations can ensure that economic security and global competitiveness go hand in hand, fostering a stable, prosperous global economy that benefits businesses, workers, and consumers alike.

Finding a Balanced Trade Strategy: Protecting American Interests While Staying Globally Competitive

Finding a balanced trade strategy is essential for ensuring that American industries remain strong, workers are protected, and the country remains competitive in the global economy. The challenge lies in achieving economic security without isolating the U.S. from international markets. Over the years, U.S. trade policy has oscillated between free trade and protectionism, with both approaches carrying advantages and drawbacks. While free trade fosters economic growth, innovation, and consumer benefits, it also increases the risks of outsourcing, trade deficits, and overreliance on foreign supply chains. On the other hand, protectionist measures like tariffs and subsidies can shield domestic industries but may also raise costs, disrupt trade relationships, and trigger retaliatory actions. A balanced trade strategy must integrate domestic industrial investment, workforce development, and strong trade agreements to ensure that the U.S. remains economically secure while engaging in global commerce.

One key component of a well-balanced trade strategy is investing in domestic industries to enhance competitiveness. Rather than using tariffs as a primary tool for economic protection, the U.S. should focus on building self-sufficiency in critical sectors such as semiconductors, clean energy, and advanced manufacturing. Programs such as the CHIPS and Science Act, which incentivizes domestic semiconductor production, are examples of how government support can reduce reliance on foreign manufacturing while fostering innovation and job creation. Additionally, clean energy investments under the Inflation

Reduction Act (IRA) promote U.S.-based production of electric vehicle batteries, solar panels, and wind turbines, ensuring that the country remains a leader in emerging industries. By strengthening domestic supply chains and boosting innovation, the U.S. can reduce its vulnerabilities without resorting to protectionist measures that disrupt trade.

A skilled workforce is another critical element of a competitive trade strategy. Many jobs that were lost to outsourcing will not return in their previous form due to advances in automation and artificial intelligence. Instead of trying to restore traditional manufacturing jobs, the U.S. must focus on upskilling workers to fill new roles in high-tech industries. Investments in STEM education, vocational training, and apprenticeship programs will help American workers transition into careers in advanced manufacturing, robotics, and digital trade. By prioritizing worker retraining and education, the U.S. can maintain a strong industrial workforce while remaining competitive in a technology-driven global economy.

At the same time, engagement in fair and strategic trade agreements is crucial for expanding U.S. market access while protecting intellectual property and fair labor standards. Rather than relying on unilateral tariffs, the U.S. should work with allies to negotiate trade deals that encourage fair competition and prevent trade distortions caused by state-subsidized industries or intellectual property theft. Strengthening partnerships with the European Union, Canada, Mexico, and Indo-Pacific nations will help the U.S. expand exports, secure access to key raw materials, and reduce reliance on economic rivals like China. Additionally, focusing on digital trade agreements, e-commerce, and technology-sharing partnerships can position the U.S. as a leader in high-value industries that drive long-term economic growth.

A balanced trade strategy must combine economic security with global engagement, ensuring that businesses, workers, and consumers all benefit from trade policies that support national prosperity while maintaining strong international partnerships. By investing in key industries, developing a skilled workforce, and negotiating fair trade agreements, the U.S. can remain globally competitive while safeguarding American interests in an increasingly interconnected economy.

Conclusion
America's Economic Future

America's economic future will be shaped by how effectively it navigates the complex challenges of global trade, industrial policy, and economic security. The trade war with China, shifts in global supply chains, and the rise of economic nationalism have forced policymakers to reconsider the balance between protectionism and globalization. While tariffs were implemented to protect domestic industries and reduce trade deficits, their long-term effects demonstrated that trade policy must be multifaceted, strategic, and adaptable to changing global conditions. The next phase of U.S. economic growth will require a forward-looking approach that integrates domestic investment, workforce development, and international cooperation to ensure sustained prosperity and global competitiveness.

One of the most significant lessons from recent trade policies is that tariffs alone cannot drive economic growth. While they provided temporary relief for some industries, they also raised costs for businesses and consumers, disrupted global supply chains, and led to retaliatory actions from trade partners. Future economic success will depend on reducing vulnerabilities in key sectors, ensuring fair competition, and strengthening domestic industrial capacity without resorting to policies that harm economic relationships. The U.S. must focus on building resilient supply chains, increasing technological innovation, and supporting high-value industries to remain competitive in a rapidly evolving global market.

Investing in domestic industries and infrastructure is critical to securing America's economic future. Programs like the CHIPS and Science Act and the Inflation Reduction Act (IRA) demonstrate the importance of government support in fostering innovation, reshoring critical manufacturing, and promoting energy independence. By incentivizing the growth of semiconductor production, clean energy technologies, and advanced manufacturing, the U.S. can reduce dependence on foreign imports and strengthen national security. However, investment must go beyond financial incentives—it must include modernizing transportation networks, improving digital infrastructure, and ensuring that businesses have access to the resources needed to compete globally.

A skilled workforce is equally essential for maintaining economic strength. Automation, artificial intelligence, and digital trade are transforming industries, requiring workers to adapt to new technologies and skill demands. America must invest in STEM education, vocational training, and apprenticeship programs to prepare workers for high-paying jobs in advanced manufacturing, clean energy, and technology sectors. Without a highly skilled labor force, the benefits of reshoring and industrial investment will be limited, as companies will continue to struggle to find qualified workers. Workforce development must be a central pillar of economic policy, ensuring that American workers remain at the forefront of technological and industrial advancements.

Finally, engaging in fair and strategic trade agreements will determine the long-term success of the U.S. economy. While economic security is important, isolationist policies and excessive protectionism can harm U.S. businesses by restricting access to foreign markets. Instead, trade agreements should focus on fair competition, intellectual property protection, and ensuring supply chain stability. Strengthening alliances with Europe, Canada, Mexico, and Indo-Pacific nations will help expand U.S. exports and maintain leadership in global trade. A balanced approach that prioritizes both economic independence and international engagement will create a more resilient, competitive, and thriving U.S. economy in the years to come.

Balancing Protectionism and Economic Growth

Balancing protectionism and economic growth is a critical challenge for policymakers as they seek to protect domestic industries while ensuring long-term prosperity. Protectionist policies, such as tariffs, subsidies, and trade restrictions, are often implemented to shield local businesses from foreign competition, reduce trade deficits, and promote domestic job creation. However, excessive protectionism can lead to higher consumer prices, supply chain disruptions, and strained international trade relations, which may ultimately hinder economic growth. On the other hand, embracing globalization without safeguards can expose industries to unfair trade practices, encourage offshoring, and weaken economic sovereignty. Striking the right balance requires a mix of strategic industrial policy, investment in innovation, workforce development, and well-negotiated trade agreements to ensure that economic growth remains sustainable while domestic industries remain competitive.

One of the primary advantages of protectionist measures is their ability to strengthen key industries and reduce reliance on foreign imports. During the U.S.-China trade war, tariffs were imposed to protect American manufacturing and reduce trade imbalances, particularly in industries such as steel, aluminum, and technology. These measures gave some domestic producers temporary relief from foreign competition, allowing them to increase production, invest in local jobs, and stabilize their markets. However, the unintended consequences of tariffs included higher costs for American businesses that relied on imported raw materials, retaliatory tariffs from trade partners, and disruptions in global supply chains. Future trade policy must take these lessons into account, ensuring that protectionist tools are used selectively and in conjunction with broader economic strategies that encourage long-term industrial growth.

A sustainable approach to economic growth involves investing in innovation, technology, and infrastructure to make domestic industries more competitive without relying heavily on tariffs. Government programs such as the CHIPS and Science Act and the Inflation Reduction Act (IRA) demonstrate the effectiveness of targeted industrial policies in promoting growth. By providing incentives for domestic semiconductor production, clean energy technology, and advanced manufacturing, these policies ensure that the U.S. remains at the forefront of emerging industries. Rather than imposing blanket tariffs, which can disrupt trade relationships, these initiatives encourage companies to invest in the U.S. voluntarily by offering economic incentives, tax credits, and research funding. Such measures reduce the risks of trade conflicts while strengthening domestic capabilities in sectors critical to national security and future economic leadership.

Another key aspect of balancing protectionism and economic growth is ensuring that the American workforce is equipped for high-skilled jobs in the evolving economy. Technological advancements, automation, and artificial intelligence have transformed industries, making it essential for workers to adapt to new skill demands. Expanding vocational training programs, STEM education, and apprenticeship opportunities will help American workers transition into high-tech manufacturing, robotics, and digital trade sectors. This approach reduces the need for protectionist policies by making U.S. labor more competitive globally, enabling companies to keep production local without sacrificing efficiency or innovation.

Ultimately, a balanced trade strategy should protect critical industries while maintaining engagement in global trade. By leveraging strategic government incentives, fostering innovation, supporting workforce development, and engaging in fair trade agreements, the U.S. can achieve sustainable economic growth without the drawbacks of extreme protectionism. The goal should be to create an economy that is resilient, competitive, and prepared for future global challenges, ensuring that American businesses and workers thrive in a rapidly changing world.

Trade Wars in the 21st Century

Trade wars in the 21st century have become a defining feature of global economic policy, reshaping international relationships, supply chains, and industrial strategies. Unlike historical trade conflicts that were primarily driven by colonial competition or resource control, modern trade wars are deeply intertwined with geopolitical power struggles, technological advancements, and economic nationalism. The U.S.-China trade war, which began in 2018, marked one of the most significant trade conflicts of the century, highlighting the risks and consequences of aggressive tariff policies. As countries navigate a rapidly changing economic landscape, trade wars have evolved into a strategic tool for economic dominance, national security, and industrial competitiveness.

One of the key drivers of modern trade wars is the competition for technological supremacy. Unlike traditional trade conflicts that focused on manufactured goods, raw materials, or agricultural products, 21st-century trade wars are centered around intellectual property, advanced technology, and digital infrastructure. The U.S. and China, for example, have clashed over issues such as semiconductors, 5G networks, artificial intelligence, and cybersecurity. The U.S. imposed restrictions on Chinese technology firms like Huawei and ZTE, citing concerns over data privacy and national security, while China has invested heavily in domestic semiconductor production to reduce reliance on U.S. and Western suppliers. This shift in trade warfare reflects the increasing importance of technology-driven economies, where controlling key innovations is just as valuable as controlling physical goods.

Another defining characteristic of 21st-century trade wars is the use of economic leverage through tariffs and sanctions. Instead of relying solely on military power or diplomatic influence, nations now use trade policies to exert economic pressure on rivals. The U.S.-China trade war saw the imposition of hundreds of billions of dollars in tariffs, affecting industries ranging from consumer electronics to agriculture. The European Union has also engaged in trade disputes with the U.S., particularly over airline subsidies, steel tariffs, and digital taxation. Meanwhile, Russia's conflict with the West following its invasion of Ukraine led to unprecedented trade sanctions, asset freezes, and energy restrictions, demonstrating how trade wars are increasingly intertwined with global security policies.

The impact of modern trade wars on global supply chains has been one of the most profound economic disruptions of the 21st century. The combination of tariffs, export bans, and retaliatory measures has forced companies to reevaluate their supply chain strategies and look for alternatives to reduce dependence on politically unstable trade routes. The COVID-19 pandemic further exposed vulnerabilities in global trade networks, prompting businesses and governments to adopt reshoring, nearshoring, and friend-shoring strategies to minimize economic risks. This shift has accelerated the regionalization of trade, with countries focusing more on self-sufficiency, economic alliances, and reduced dependency on traditional rivals.

Moving forward, trade wars in the 21st century will likely continue to be shaped by technological advancements, national security concerns, and shifting global alliances. While tariffs and sanctions may remain a favored economic tool, the emphasis will increasingly be on controlling emerging technologies, securing critical raw materials, and building resilient trade partnerships. Nations that can effectively balance economic protectionism with global cooperation will be best positioned to navigate the complexities of modern trade warfare and maintain long-term economic stability.

www.ingramcontent.com/pod-product-compliance
Lightning Source LLC
LaVergne TN
LVHW061552070526
838199LV00077B/7017